Bob Dylan

Forever Young

LIFE Books

Managing Editor Robert Sullivan
Director of Photography Barbara Baker Burrows
Creative Director Mimi Park
Deputy Picture Editor Christina Lieberman
Copy Editors Parlan McGaw (Chief), Barbara Gogan
Writer-Reporters Michelle DuPré (Chief), Marilyn Fu
Photo Associate Sarah Cates
Consulting Picture Editors Mimi Murphy (Rome),
Tala Skari (Paris)
Special thanks to Dave Brolan and to Aaron Zych and
the Morrison Hotel Gallery

Editorial Operations Richard K. Prue (Director),
Brian Fellows (Manager), Keith Aurelio, Charlotte Coco,
Kevin Hart, Mert Kerimoglu, Rosalie Khan, Patricia Koh,
Marco Lau, Brian Mai, Po Fung Ng, Rudi Papiri,
Robert Pizaro, Barry Pribula, Clara Renauro, Katy Saunders,
Samantha Schwendaman, Hia Tan, Vaune Trachtman

TIME HOME ENTERTAINMENT

Publisher Richard Fraiman
Vice President, Business Development & Strategy Steven Sandonato
Executive Director, Marketing Services Carol Pittard
Executive Director, Retail & Special Sales Tom Mifsud
Executive Publishing Director Joy Butts
Director Bookazine Development & Marketing Laura Adam
Finance Director Glenn Buonocore
Associate Publishing Director Megan Pearlman
Assistant General Counsel Helen Wan
Assistant Director, Special Sales Ilene Schreider
Book Production Manager Suzanne Janso
Design & Prepress Manager Anne-Michelle Gallero
Brand Manager Roshni Patel
Associate Prepress Manager Alex Voznesenskiy
Assistant Brand Manager Stephanie Braga

Editorial Director Stephen Koepp
Editorial Operations Director Michael Q. Bullerdick

Special thanks to Christine Austin, Katherine Barnet, Jeremy Biloon,
Jim Childs, Susan Chodakiewicz, Rose Cirrincione, Lauren Hall Clark,
Jacqueline Fitzgerald, Christine Font, Jenna Goldberg, Hillary Hirsch,
David Kahn, Amy Mangus, Robert Marasco, Kimberly Marshall, Amy
Migliaccio, Nina Mistry, Dave Rozzelle, Adriana Tierno, Vanessa Wu

ISBN 10: 1-60320-060-6
ISBN 13: 978-1-60320-060-8
Library of Congress Control Number: 2011945647

"LIFE" is a registered trademark of Time Inc.

We welcome your comments and suggestions
about LIFE Books. Please write to us at:
LIFE Books, Attention: Book Editors
PO Box 11016, Des Moines, IA 50336-1016

If you would like to order any of our hardcover Collector's
Edition books, please call us at: 1-800-327-6388
(7 a.m.–8 p.m. Monday to Friday, or
7 a.m.–6 p.m. Saturday, Central Time).

Page 1: Not quite riding in New York City in
1965. PHOTOGRAPH BY DANIEL KRAMER

Pages 2–3: In 1968, Dylan and his son
Jesse are spending time outside the family
home in Byrdcliffe, New York.
PHOTOGRAPH BY ELLIOTT LANDY/MAGNUM

These pages: Joan Baez, Arlo Guthrie,
Ramblin' Jack Elliott and Bob Dylan at the
Dream Away Lodge in Becket, Massachusetts,
in 1975, filming a scene that will end up in
the unfortunate *Renaldo and Clara*.
PHOTOGRAPH BY KEN REGAN/CAMERA 5

Endpapers: The folksinger in 1963.
PHOTOGRAPHS BY DON HUNSTEIN

Contents

6   **Introduction: Our Dylan**

8   **Birth of a Folksinger**

34   **Inspirations**

36   **Plugging In**

58   **Dylan and the Band**

60   **Retreat, Return**

78   **Dylan at the Movies**

80   **Rolling On**

96   **Just One More**

Introduction

Our Dylan

We've done a lot of books here at LIFE Books, and we certainly do enjoy putting each of them together, whether the subject is the world's wonders, a glamorous star of Hollywood's golden age, a royal wedding, the sinking of the *Titanic* or the daring mission that took out Osama bin Laden. The interests and passions of our staff are various, and so we really do relish digging into whatever topic can be presented well in pictures and narrative.

When we decided to "do" Bob Dylan, the enthusiasm in the office ratcheted up a notch beyond its high normal. All of us had thoughts on and feelings about Dylan. All of us were pretty clear-eyed about what a difficult (*obstreperous* is a good word, *cantankerous* is another) character he has been at times. But all of us appreciated what he has meant to us at other times, when we were listening closely as the records played.

Our photo chief, Bobbi, immediately said "Ken," knowing she wanted to get in touch with her friend Ken Regan for the extraordinary photography from the Rolling Thunder Revue tour (in which period, just by the way, Caroline Kennedy served as Ken's assistant at various points), and also her friend Elliott Landy, for the intimate Woodstock material. Our deputy photo chief, Christina, who I'm guessing possessed a bootlegged copy of the Dylan memoir even before it was published, was established as our Palace Guard on all things we might say about the former Bobby Zimmerman, and she brought in Jim Marshall's and Dan Kramer's wonderful pictures. Our younger staff—Sarah and Marilyn and Michelle—were delighted to learn more about this guy who was important to their parents and, as it turns out, themselves. Their e-mails with queries about one fine point or another routinely started with, "This Dylan guy is really something!" So they were learning his detailed biography for the first time, but he—as a

thing, an American thing—was already a touchstone. Michelle, a poet, said that she had always been a fan of Dylan's "amazing writing." Marilyn, a prize-winning screenwriter who is nonetheless quite as young as young can be, sounded like a Greenwich Village coffeehouse habitué, circa 1962, when she said, "His music spoke to me most during a more carefree time when my entire day could actually be spent sitting around with friends, listening to Dylan and having a conversation."

Mimi, who designed our book, shared that sentiment, having been sucked in by Scorsese's documentary. Our copy editor Parlan, a dyed-in-the-wool Dylanist (he's seen him in concert four times), is also a professional actor and acting teacher, and so of course was fascinated by the public Dylan: What was a mask, what wasn't? Our other copy editor, Barbara, happens to be a rock star in her own right: She was the lead singer in the British new wave band the Passions, whose 1981 hit "I'm in Love with a German Film Star" is still remembered fondly by thousands beyond Barbara's colleagues at LIFE, and was covered in recent years by the Foo Fighters and then the Pet Shop Boys. Barbara told us a little story: "I remember a Thanksgiving dinner years ago with some very intelligent people, most of whom I didn't know well. And the question was asked, 'Whose death would fundamentally shift your sense of being in the world?' Bob Dylan was the resounding winner."

Dylan in Bangor, Maine, during the early days of the Rolling Thunder Revue tour in 1975.

Well, he hasn't won yet, because he certainly hasn't died. He's still very much out there, playing night after night to the old and young, while continuing to make relevant, sensational (and chart-topping) new music. His last two studio albums of original material have both gone to Number One—more than a half century after he arrived in New York City from Minnesota and started bumming and strumming in the Village.

I was a Beatles kid and came to Dylan just a little later, but became a thoroughgoing fan once I found him. I first saw him play in Lowell, Massachusetts, in 1975, during one of the early Rolling Thunder Revue shows. I had already seen the Band at that point, and Springsteen at my college (a half-filled auditorium, by the way), but I had never felt such magic emanate from a stage. I know that sounds a bit much, and I am quite ready to leaven it; I well realize that Dylan is no transcendent god; he is, as he himself has often argued, just a guy with a trade. I caught the Rolling Thunder Revue again closer to the end of its run, and although Springsteen and Joni Mitchell guested, the show wasn't a patch on what Dylan had accomplished when he was fired up in Lowell. Later still, in Providence, Rhode Island, I attended one of his born-again shows, and remember him arguing with the sparse audience about Jesus and God as he once had about whether a guitar should be plugged in or not. So many sides of this multisided man, in just three concerts: the contrariness, the seeking, the great music, the insistent music, the petulant music, the poetic, the strident, the caring, the uncaring, the generous, the less than generous, the self-centered, the self-giving.

The world at large should end its 50-year hunt: There will never be a new Dylan. While we have him, we can celebrate the real thing.

As for us at LIFE Books, well, from the very first, we knew that we just *had* to do Dylan.

—ROBERT SULLIVAN

Birth of a Folksinger

The prodigious Minnesotan Robert Zimmerman, who certainly hoped that one day books would be written about him, just as certainly never imagined—even in his considerable ambition and his wildest dreams—that there would be so many such books. And he surely never guessed that one of them might start with a note about Roger Maris and Kevin McHale—guys he certainly didn't know.

Bobby Zimmerman was born in Duluth on May 24, 1941, but the legend of his extraordinary life usually begins with Hibbing, a smaller place that was his mother's hometown (his grandparents, both maternal and paternal, were Jewish immigrants from Europe, and his people were ensconced in Minnesota's small but tight-knit Jewish community). His family had relocated when Bobby was six after his father, Abe, contracted polio and the Zimmermans required a support system. Whatever trauma the boy or his toddler brother, David, might have felt at the time remains unplumbed; it's just the kind of subject that Bob Dylan sloughs off. And maybe he is right to do so, for his childhood seems to have been happy enough. He went to school, he did okay, he liked rock 'n' roll. When he wasn't yet a teenager, his parents allowed him and his friends to practice in the garage, though Beatrice Zimmerman was forced to intercede when Mrs. Schleppegrell from across the street asked politely if the boys couldn't keep it down a bit because it was her son Bill's nap time. While at Hibbing High, Bobby performed in the Shadow Blasters, and then the Golden Chords, whose amped-up performance of the Danny and the Juniors song "Rock and Roll Is Here to Stay" so unnerved the high school principal that he terminated their performance at the school's talent show. As was the case with many would-be rockers in the late 1950s, Zimmerman and his bandmates were constantly being told to turn down the volume—either by their parents, their neighbors or the authorities.

The cap, the guitar, the harmonica rack: All would become signature items after the college dropout from the Midwest hit the Big Apple, leaving not only his hometown but his old self, Bobby Zimmerman, behind.

Hibbing's population when the Zimmermans landed there just after World War II was about 16,300—almost precisely what it is today. Located about 70 miles northwest of Duluth, it was and remains an industrial city/town; on its outskirts is the largest open-pit iron mine in the world. People worked hard there. Kids played sandlot ball and shot hoops for hours on end at the schoolyard. If some young people might emerge to carry the banner of Hibbing forward to the wider world, they might be such as native son Maris, who is still rightfully regarded as Major League Baseball's all-time single-season home run king. Or they might be such as McHale, who would grow very tall and would win NBA basketball championships alongside Larry Bird in Boston. In Hibbing, you could practice baseball and basketball often enough to develop your skills.

But to come out of Hibbing and become an iconoclastic singer and songwriter—his name mentioned, in the latter pursuit, with such American legends as Berlin, Gershwin, Porter and Guthrie—to become a Pulitzer Prize honoree, to become one of the world's titanic cultural figures of the 20th and early 21st centuries . . . Well, that was less than unlikely. It was impossible. For that to happen, the individual would have to be a genius.

And Hibbing is the first evidence offered when people assert confidently: "Bob Dylan is a genius."

Top: Bobby, about two years old, sits before his mom, the former Beatrice Stone, who was called Beatty (said: *B.T.*) by her friends, in the farthest right mother-child pairing. Above is one of the boy's childhood homes, at 2425 7th Avenue in Hibbing, a street since renamed Bob Dylan Drive. Opposite: He's already standing out in a crowd in his first grade class at Hibbing's Alice School. Sixth from left, top row, he's the boy looking away.

He is that, no doubt.

He was probably born a genius. Just as certainly, he has always been ambitious, restless, open to experiment, self-aware, ornery, provocative and tireless. Let's put "inscrutable" and "incomprehensible" aside this time. He's pretty scrutable, if one accepts his screwiness. And if one dismisses the nonsense that he has enjoyed disgorging in the relatively rare interviews he has given through the years, he's comprehensible—just listen to his songs. Dylan plays games, no doubt about it; he always has. And the game-playing tends to obscure his seriousness of purpose. He becomes "the jester" in Don McLean's lyrical survey of American postwar music, "American Pie," and yet at the end of the day the jester will have delivered a veritable canon of indelible songs, and will have performed, sometimes unevenly, for a gazillion people—more, certainly, than any jester in history. He is still on the road on his Never-Ending Tour, a half century after leaving Minnesota and landing in Greenwich Village, having changed his surname from Zimmerman to Dylan along the way. As you read these words, people are filing into a Bob Dylan concert somewhere—in Anaheim or Zurich, in Boston or Berlin or, now, Beijing.

He has traveled a long, long road from Hibbing, without looking back and with, as he and the documentarians have also said, no direction home.

From an October 20, 1963, *Duluth News Tribune* article by staff writer Walter Eldot: "There's an unwritten code in show business that people like to be deceived. Performers, therefore, must be legendized and molded into a public image that is often quite different from what they used to be.

"It happened to Bobby Zimmerman from Hibbing—now widely known as Bob Dylan, 22, folksinger and songwriter.

"His rise in barely three years has been almost as impressive as the considerable fortune he has already amassed, the character he has assumed, the reams of reviews and stories written about him, and his Carnegie Hall debut next Saturday.

"Who and what is Bob Dylan?"

Well asked, Mr. Eldot—even unto "the character he has assumed"—a question we are still asking a half century later.

Eldot and particularly the locals in Hibbing would have remembered the Golden Chords kid who was better than most, who had played dates with the touring pop star Bobby Vee, adding handclaps and a touch of piano. By the time of the Carnegie Hall breakthrough, these locals were repairing to Bob's senior year high school yearbook, where he had written that his ambition was "To join 'Little Richard.'" Maybe they remembered, some of them, that he had been Echo Helstrom's boyfriend for about a year. She was a beautiful blonde from the poorer side of town, and may later have been the inspiration

GAYLE STEVENS, JOYCE KELLY & BOB HOCKING

Below: Bobby is on percussion in fifth grade music class (he's seated, at right). Right: An ad for an upcoming Golden Chords show. A couple of things worth noting: Alphabetical order being cruel for surnames starting with Z, young master Zimmerman is billed last. Also, this snippet from a *Hibbing Tribune* edition of 1958 is a record of Bob Dylan's first-ever paid show; his fellow Chord, LeRoy Hoikkala, has said that Bobby told him on the way to the gig that, until this rock 'n' roll hop, he had always obligingly played for free. Opposite: The teenage front man is resplendent in a 1958 portrait taken at home by his mom. Do take note: His Sears Danelectro Silvertone guitar is a very plugged-in model indeed.

- -

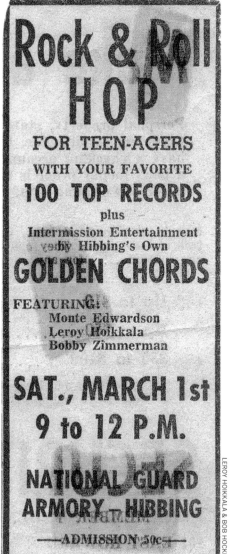

for "Girl from the North Country" and songs on *Blonde on Blonde*. Be that as it may—and Dylan, who called this girl "Becky Thatcher" in *Chronicles: Volume One*, will never fess up—she was important to Bobby, in several ways. "One of the reasons I liked going there [to Echo's house] besides puppy love, was that they had Jimmie Rodgers records, old 78's in the house," Dylan wrote. So he liked the fact that folks were comparing Echo to Brigitte Bardot, but he liked this as well.

Maybe there had been clues in Hibbing regarding talents and tendencies, the ability to sing and the ability to learn and absorb. But, still, how had Bobby Zimmerman pulled this off in New York, if not by dint of genius? The folks back home didn't have a clue.

"But Dylan is essentially a self-made creation," Eldot wrote, "right down to the name which he borrowed from Dylan Thomas, the Welsh poet whose writings he likes, and some of the things he does strictly for effect.

"'My son is a corporation and his public image is strictly an act,' says his father."

What Abe, who worked in Hibbing as an appliance and furniture dealer, and Beatrice Zimmerman knew about their older boy at that point was that he was a little different—not dangerously much, but a little. They had bought their boys a piano in hopes that they would like music, but had no idea where this preternatural talent came from. They knew he liked to listen to the radio, and they probably didn't wonder that his choice of fare included blues, country and early rock 'n' roll being broadcast from as far away as the Mississippi Delta. In fact, his dad put up an antenna to allow for better reception. They were aware that Bobby had always been interested in poetry and stories; they had saved compositions he had written as early as age eight. The Zimmermans told Eldot that they realized when he was still a boy "that Bobby had a real streak of talent, but we didn't know what kind. We just could not corral it." They would not be the last to make that observation.

Part of the legend is that their son ran away six times before his famous flight for New York City, his seventh and final departure. But that's part of the legend: He was a restless

kid, but not a bad one, and when he headed east after barely a year at the University of Minnesota in Minneapolis, it was with his parents' foreknowledge. "He had as many friends as he wanted [at college] but he considered most of them phonies—spoiled kids with whom he didn't feel he had much in common," his father told the *News Tribune*. "He wanted to have free reign. He wanted to be a folksinger, an entertainer. We couldn't see it, but we felt he was entitled to the chance. It's his life, after all, and we didn't want to stand in the way. So we made an agreement that he could have one year to do as he pleased, and if at the end of that year we were not satisfied with his progress he'd go back to school." It was precisely the kind of mutually respectful bargain a million and more young people have made with their parents through the ages, and if it doesn't fit so conveniently with the boho/rebel/beatnik story of the soon-to-be-invented Bob Dylan, so be it. At least Mr. Zimmerman admitted that his son probably did hitchhike his way east, rather than take a bus or train: "He got himself a ride to New York."

What had built Bob's surety that he had to go, and that he

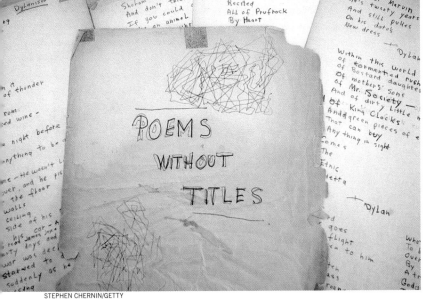

Opposite: He always enjoyed motorcycles, and indeed one of them would play a central role, and lead to a crucial interlude, in his life and career. But when he and his pal Dale Boutang are happy young teens in Hibbing posing with a Harley in 1956, there is no crashing being done. The "Poems Without Titles" are written in 1960. The previous year he has graduated from high school, and the yearbook says what you need to know: He wants to be a rock star, and is into social studies. In 1963, Bob Dylan will write a poem: "Hibbing's got souped-up cars runnin' full blast on a Friday night / Hibbing's got corner bars with polka bands / You can stand at one end of Hibbing's main drag an' see clear past the city limits on the other end / Hibbing's a good ol' town."

Barbara Yeshe

Robert Zimmerman

Shirley Zubich

Stephen LeDoux

"WE'LL REMEMBER ALWAYS..."

Barbara Yeshe: not for long—F.N.A. 3, 4; F.H.A. 2, 3; F.B.L.A. 4; Schubert Chorus 2; Pep Club 2.

Robert Zimmerman: to join "Little Richard"—Latin Club 2; Social Studies Club 4.

Shirley Zubich: not least, but usually last—F.N.A. 3, 4; F.B.L.A. 3, 4; Masquers 3, 4; Social Studies Club 4; Pep Club 4; Girls' League 3; Jr.-Sr. Prom Committee 3; "Stag Line" production 3.

Stephen LeDoux: to do better with each passing day—

Margaret Spinelli: forever having her seat changed—F.B.L.A. 3; Jr. Red Cross 3; Pep Club 2, 3; Girls' League 2; Jr.-Sr. Prom Committee 3.

Taking the Village (and the city) by storm: At left, he is just another folkie spinning his discs. But soon he is noticed: In September 1961, Robert Shelton of *The New York Times* catches his act at Gerdes Folk City in Greenwich Village (opposite) and writes a gushing review. Meantime, the good folks at the Folklore Center, having seen him perform at the Bitter End and elsewhere, arrange for a proper uptown concert in Carnegie Chapter Hall (below). He is well on his way, and his first album hasn't even been released!

might find success where he was heading? Well, at university, where it had been thought he would concentrate on the liberal arts and science, young Zimmerman had instead found himself spending his time in a pizza joint, where he sang and played guitar and harmonica for his fellow students. In this period, he was drifting from Danny and the Juniors to the blues and the Weavers, as he later explained: "The thing about rock 'n' roll is that for me anyway it wasn't enough . . . [T]he songs weren't serious or didn't reflect life in a realistic way. I knew that when I got into folk music, it was more of a serious type of thing. The songs are filled with more despair, more sadness, more triumph, more faith in the supernatural, much deeper feelings." He added gigs at the Ten O'Clock Scholar, a bona fide coffee house, to the pizza-place stints, and began introducing himself occasionally by his latterly famous stage name. In the summer of 1959 he met, in Denver, the noted African American bluesman Jesse Fuller, who was something of a one-man band—singing while accompanying himself on guitar, kazoo and a harmonica held in a rack. Zimmerman borrowed this last bit, as he would borrow much through the years. He later paid tribute by covering a Jesse Fuller song on his debut album.

In January 1961, Bobby Zimmerman, who was at the time remembered back in Hibbing as the rock 'n' roll kid silenced by the principal—if he was remembered at all—arrived in New York City as Bob Dylan, an anonymous folkie determined never to be quieted again. He was also determined to visit the man who had become his musical idol, Woody Guthrie, writer of "This Land Is Your Land" and scores of other popular songs, a man Dylan felt was "the true voice of the American spirit. I said to myself I was going to be Guthrie's greatest disciple." He did see Guthrie at his bedside in the Greystone Park Psychiatric Hospital, where the

THE FOLKLORE CENTER

Presents

BOB DYLAN

IN HIS FIRST NEW YORK CONCERT

SAT. NOV. 4, 1961   8:40pm

CARNEGIE CHAPTER HALL

154 WEST 57th STREET • NEW YORK CITY

All seats $2.00

Tickets available at: The Folklore Center
                          110 MacDougal Street
GR 7 - 5987   New York City 12, New York

Dylan had *hoped* life in the big city would treat him kindly, but this is ridiculous. He suddenly has all these new, talented friends. Below he performs with the Greenbriar Boys, Ralph Rinzler (left) and John Herald, at the Gaslight club in 1962. At bottom, he is with Ramblin' Jack Elliott, who would remain a constant buddy, joining Dylan more than 10 years later on the Rolling Thunder Revue tour. At right, he and Dave Van Ronk are escorts on the happy streets of the Village. The young woman with Dylan is Suze Rotolo, and she is important. On the pages following, we learn more about her.

storied folksinger and author (memoir: *Bound for Glory*) was gravely ill with Huntington's disease. He played songs for Woody, and Woody was gracious in his thanks. These audiences that Dylan was granted would become part of the lore once the young man from Minnesota began to be noticed,

which happened very fast.

Within a month of hitting the city, Dylan was singing in clubs in and near Greenwich Village. There was astonishingly little toil and trouble to his rise; in Dylan's case, the term *meteoric* really does apply.

To read Dylan's own memoir, *Chronicles: Volume One*, and other books dealing with the times as they were a-changing, life was exciting on a daily basis among the young and footloose in the early 1960s. Sure, they were upset about civil rights issues, inequalities and, soon enough, the masters of

In the postcard, Dylan writes from Rome to his girlfriend back home, Suze. When he is back in their shared Greenwich Village apartment, there is pretty good (or not too bad) plonk, and quiet time to think about the future—the future of the world, future songs waiting to be written, their own futures. Both of these photographs were made in January 1962—Dylan's first album now just weeks away.

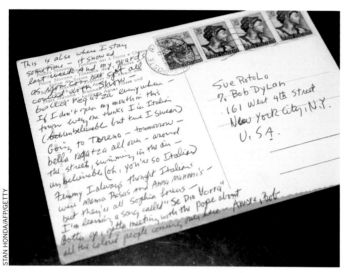

war. But they were free and easy, they were on their own, and for those of them like Dylan, who communicated from the stage, applause was a nightly guarantee. That's pretty heady; that's pretty good. There were few or none who emerged from that scene who ever looked back with regret. It was quite a moment.

Dylan was drinking it all in, soaking it all up. His friend from the early days, the folksinger Dave Van Ronk, recalled in *No Direction Home* (the Martin Scorsese documentary about Dylan) and on many other occasions that there was no greater sponge than Dylan. He adopted the stylings of others, the inflections of blues singers who had gone before. In short order he would be borrowing bits of melody: from the slave song "No More Auction Block" for "Blowin' in the Wind," from the traditional ballad "Lord Randall" for "A Hard Rain's A-Gonna Fall." He stole a friend's records because, as he himself admitted to Scorsese much later, he simply had to have them. Having them was essential. In the melting pot that was Bob Dylan, all of this, mixed with his own individual brilliance, produced something truly special, if only sometimes likeable.

Once the folkies and folk fans had returned to the Village from their summer festival outposts in September of 1961, the buzz was strong. That month, two things happened that set the young performer on his course. Dylan performed at Gerdes Folk City and Robert Shelton, with whom Dylan would much later cooperate on a biography, wrote a positive

Now the album has come out, the fame game is in force, and soft moments lounging in the apartment are fewer, while formal photo sessions are more frequent. These photographs, most obviously the charming shot of Suze and Bob at right, are all from the session that produced the famous cover of his second album, *The Freewheelin' Bob Dylan*.

review in *The New York Times*. Dylan and his friends, reading Shelton's appraisal, must have felt precisely as Jack Kerouac and his pals had four years earlier, when Gilbert Millstein had declared *On the Road* to be a book to which attention must be paid. Even back in Hibbing, the importance of the review registered. "We figured that anybody who can get his picture and two columns in *The New York Times* is doing pretty good," said Abe Zimmerman, who surely knew at this point that his kid wasn't going back to college anytime soon. "Anyway, it was a start."

Meantime, that same September, Dylan was hired to play harmonica on folksinger Carolyn Hester's new album, which she was recording with producer John Hammond for release on Columbia Records. Hammond, already a legendary kingmaker in the recording industry (he had boosted the careers of Benny Goodman, Billie Holiday and Pete Seeger among

others, and would sign Bruce Springsteen and Stevie Ray Vaughan in the years to come), offered Dylan a deal immediately, and the artist's eponymous first album was released early the following year. A collection of mostly covers of traditional songs (there were two Dylan compositions: "Talkin' New York" and "Song to Woody," which featured a melody based on Guthrie's own "1913 Massacre"), the record initially sold fewer than 5,000 copies. Folks at Columbia thought that their Svengali of a producer had, in a rare act, stubbed his toe. They called the kid from Minnesota "Hammond's Folly."

Dylan was unfazed. He was writing songs a mile a minute now, several of them based on tunes that had been blowing on the breeze long before Bobby Zimmerman's birth. (Adding to his reputation as a pilferer along Bleecker Street, he had taken claim on his first album for an arrangement of "House of the Risin' Sun" that was Van Ronk's, something Van Ronk

would joke about—sort of—for decades.) The original material fell into two categories: message, or protest, songs and then that old standby, the love song. A young woman named Suze Rotolo was an influence on both kinds. She was the daughter—born in Brooklyn, raised in Queens—of two card-carrying American Communists and was, while in high school, working as an activist for both the Congress of Racial Equality and the anti-nuke group SANE. She had met Dylan at a concert at Riverside Church in the summer of 1961, and Dylan would later write in his memoirs: "Right from the start I couldn't take my eyes off her. She was the most erotic thing I'd ever seen. She was fair skinned and golden haired, full-blood Italian. The air was suddenly filled with banana leaves. We started talking and my head started to spin. Cupid's arrow had whistled past my ears before, but this time it hit me in the heart and the weight of it dragged me overboard."

Yes, well, that was a good thing for all of us Dylan fans, as his romance with Suze (they moved in together, into an apartment on West 4th Street, in January 1962) directly inspired the songs "Don't Think Twice, It's All Right," "Tomorrow Is a Long Time," "One Too Many Mornings" and "Boots of Spanish Leather." How much her liberal political views made

their way into his topical songs has been speculated upon endlessly, but it's probable that there's as much Suze Rotolo as Pete Seeger or Woody Guthrie in "Oxford Town," "Blowin' in the Wind," "Masters of War" and "A Hard Rain's A-Gonna Fall." She was everything to him, for a time.

If you don't think you know her, you do. She is the happy young woman clinging to her boyfriend's arm as they walk down the slushy Greenwich Village street on the cover of the boyfriend's second album, *The Freewheelin' Bob Dylan*. While he was recording what would be his breakthrough record, he was continuing to climb in reputation—he landed that first

The summer of '63 is crucial to Dylan's gaining a foothold in the national consciousness. He wows them at Newport (left). He is an accepted member of folk's royalty for the group sing (from left, below, Peter, Mary, Paul, Joan, Bob). And he is at work on the songs that will fill his first album of all-original material and establish him as a songwriter for all to reckon with. Bottom, the lyrics in manuscript for what will become the title song of that album, and quickly an anthem: "The Times They Are A-Changin'" He is in the studio recording before the summer is out.

‑ ‑

ROWLAND SCHERMAN

© JIM MARSHALL PHOTOGRAPHY

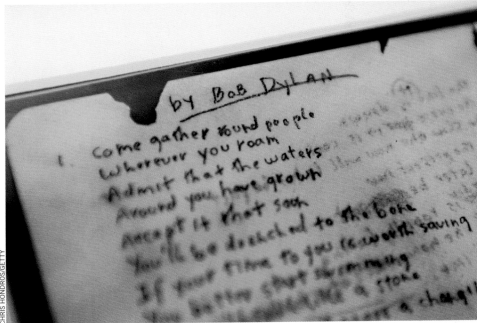

CHRIS HONDROS/GETTY

© JIM MARSHALL PHOTOGRAPHY

No, this (left) is not their love child, it's someone else's kid. Nonetheless, in the folk world and beyond, it is now an open secret that Joan and Bob are a pair. As Suze Rotolo influenced Dylan politically, so does Baez. But he keeps his eyes on his personal prize. He tells a friend at one point that he wrote "The Times They Are A-Changin'" because it was what he thought people wanted to hear. And when he celebrates with Joan (below, left) it's because he's in love and his career is soaring, not necessarily because he's saving the world. Meantime, all the time, he keeps working. Below: Writing lyrics while being driven to a concert in Philadelphia.

PHOTOGRAPHS © DANIEL KRAMER (2)

Carnegie Hall gig, which forced even the newspaper back in Duluth to take notice—but he was, for a time, bereft. Suze didn't enjoy being seen as an appendage (she said the musicians' girlfriends in the Village scene were perceived as "chicks," and she was smarter than that), and with her mother's support, she left New York for an extended sojourn in Italy. She returned to New York, and to Dylan, in January 1963, but everything was to become much more complicated by the success of *Freewheelin'*, Dylan's ascendancy in the world of pop culture, and—not least—the singer's love affair with Joan Baez.

Baez was already nationally famous; Dylan was about to be. Until this point, his voice was holding him back from the big break.

Critics and the masses have, these several decades later, generally acknowledged that Dylan's vocals are compelling in the extreme, but for the radio audience back at that time, they were, shall we say, something of an acquired taste. His singing voice was nasal, to be sure, and, if emotive, raw. Baez's, by contrast, was ethereal and seemingly effortless. The folksingers Peter, Paul and Mary had lovely voices as well, and pop groups including the Byrds, the Turtles, and Sonny and Cher all had easily accessible sounds—and all had big hits with Bob Dylan songs. The songwriter's own record label reacted defensively at one point with a "Nobody Sings Dylan Like Dylan" campaign, but Baez took a different tack, inviting him onstage as a surprise guest at her appearances, including the big one at the Newport Folk Festival in 1963, to prove the point live.

Public appearances that year, as much as the fine reviews received by *Freewheelin'*, served to define and position Dylan. In May, he was defined and positioned as well by an appearance that didn't happen. Dylan had written one of his satirical

Dylan did *care*, certainly; it simply cannot have been otherwise. Just after the Fourth of July in 1963, he and fellow star folksingers Pete Seeger (below) and Theodore Bikel make their way, at personal danger, to Greenwood, Mississippi, for a voter registration rally. Dylan sings in an open field (left) and on the back porch of the local Student Nonviolent Coordinating Committee office (opposite). He performs "Only a Pawn in Their Game," about the murder of the Mississippi NAACP leader Medgar Evers—one of the new songs he is assembling for that next, different album. Bernice Johnson is working for the cause at the time, and she will later tell biographer Robert Shelton, "'Pawn' was the very first song that showed the poor white was as victimized by discrimination as the poor black. The Greenwood people didn't know that Pete, Theo and Bobby were well known. They were just happy to be getting support. But they really like Dylan down there in the cotton country."

----

songs about an ultraconservative group that held a certain sway at the time, the John Birch Society. He was in rehearsal for an eagerly anticipated segment on *The Ed Sullivan Show*, a gig that would greatly increase his profile, when he was told that CBS's "head of Standards and Practices," fearing a libel suit by the political organization, had nixed "Talkin' John Birch Paranoid Blues." Rather than change his set list, Dylan walked. While he was denied the huge Sunday night audience that would, the next year, help launch the Beatles' invasion of America, he gained massive credibility with the left-leaning folkie crowd.

Then came Newport at Baez's side, where Dylan was rapturously received. He was the new folk prince, and she was his patroness. Suze Rotolo accompanied Dylan to Newport, not knowing (or not quite sure) that he and Joan were lovers. Once she was there and once she was certain, she left the relationship, only to learn that she was pregnant. She and Dylan arranged for an illegal abortion "through friends," according to Rotolo in her memoir, with what they considered "a good doctor."

Dylan, meanwhile, in his constantly calculating way, realized that his audience was largely New York and now Newport, while Baez's was national and potentially global. He was happy to agree to be her "special guest" on her now-starting tour. On August 28, Dylan and Baez were together at the March on Washington for Jobs and Freedom. They sang; Martin Luther King Jr. delivered his "I Have a Dream Speech"; and suddenly Dylan was being talked of as one of the seminal voices of his generation. This perception was

solidified with the release of his third album, *The Times They Are A-Changin'*, which, with the exception of two love songs remaining from his bygone relationship with Suze Rotolo, was political top to bottom. Civil rights, economic inequity, the travails of mine workers: You name it, Bob took it on.

So now we knew for sure exactly who Bob Dylan was: a socially conscious folksinger ready to fight for the working man, the oppressed, all that was wrong with the world.

The problem was: That wasn't how he saw himself, and he was about to let his fans know it.

In interviews, he began to sound contrarian at best and often crackpot. We will dwell in our next chapter at a little more length on his classic, super-surrealistic *Playboy* interview of 1966—still ranked by *New York* magazine at Number One on its list of Ten Most Incomprehensible Bob Dylan Interviews of All Time—but suffice for now: Dylan began

publicly denying the mantle that had been *thrust* upon him, regardless of the fact that he had so assiduously, even cunningly, campaigned for that mantle. He didn't write "message" songs, he insisted, and he didn't speak for any generation. His new cantankerousness was unappealing to say the least. Many defenders would get used to it over time, and he himself would leaven it over time, saying that he really *did* like his fans but that he couldn't be responsible for them. But the crankiness

of '63 was new, and reached its nadir near year's end when he deigned to accept the Tom Paine Award from the Emergency Civil Liberties Committee: a trophy, in other words, for something he was now denying he deserved. Why he showed up at the Americana Hotel and behaved so abominably, only three weeks after John F. Kennedy's assassination, is, like with many things involving Bob Dylan, anyone's guess. But show up he did. If he wasn't already drunk when he arrived, he soon

TED RUSSELL/POLARIS

ROWLAND SCHERMAN/GETTY

With Baez as his patroness, 1963 is a heady ride for Dylan, including a performance at her side at the civil rights rally in Washington, D.C., on August 28. But late in the year, there is rougher sailing. Above: The esteemed writer James Baldwin seems as bewildered as anyone else by Dylan's condition, behavior and words during the Tom Paine Award ceremony in New York City on December 13.

became so, in the estimation of most in attendance. In his "acceptance" speech he laid into the Committee's mission and its membership, which was made up, after all, of old, bald guys ("I'm proud that I'm young. And I only wish that all you people who are sitting out here today or tonight weren't here and I could see all kinds of faces with hair on their head"). He certainly gladdened the hearts of all in his audience when he continued that he saw parts of Lee Harvey Oswald in himself.

You can imagine how that played back in Hibbing.

Many who know Dylan well say that he is a sensitive, shy, often insecure guy, and this is not to be doubted. He was no doubt pained by the reaction to his appearance at the Tom Paine Award function, and quickly apologized. But he was about to choose personal and artistic paths for which he would not say "I'm sorry," and for which there was no need to.

The folkies didn't know or care that he had once dug Danny and the Juniors, and if now he was heading back that way—well, that wasn't their business. Except that they thought it was. He recorded *Another Side of Bob Dylan* on a single night in 1964, and if his listeners didn't understand that "It Ain't Me, Babe" wasn't written just to a woman, well, they should have. In March 1965, he released *Bringing It All Back Home*, which despite its woodsy title featured his first forays into electric backing; "Subterranean Homesick Blues" stands today as a bridge from Chuck Berry to hip-hop. The fans were getting worried, and Dylan didn't help them out. His frizzy hair was grown ever outward, the sunglasses were now worn day and night, the jeans were skintight and the footwear transitioned to Beatle boots. Beatle boots!

The revered prince of rebellion, the voice of the revolution, was starting to rebel against what it was thought he stood for.

He was about to turn the volume up—way up.

- -

Now, in 1964, Dylan is squarely in the center of the spotlight—and it will remain this way the rest of his days. Not only does he no longer have to lean on anyone for support or advice, he is insistent that this is now his show, from lights-up until curtain call, and if he has any guests on stage it will be by very special invitation. To be sure: Dylan will accept all responsibility for whatever outcome awaits. If the audience rejects him for no longer being a duo with Baez, then the audience rejects him. If the audience rejects him for fronting a former roadhouse band who play at a higher decibel level, then the audience rejects him. If, several years down the road, the audience rejects him for loaning out his famous "message" songs for Madison Avenue ad campaigns, then the audience rejects him. He was on his own when he made his way from Hibbing to New York City, and now, as he prepares to take another plunge, he's on his own again. Judging by what we know about Bob Dylan, 50 years on, this is the way he likes it. And always has.

Inspirations

As we have said, Dylan soaked up everything he saw or heard: how to sing, how to play, how to write, how to perform. His influences range from white-bread '50s pop bands to soulful Depression-era African American folksingers, from the fiercest rock 'n' rollers to traditional acoustic-guitar balladeers. Herewith, pieces of Dylan.

MICHAEL OCHS ARCHIVES/GETTY

ABC PHOTO ARCHIVES/GETTY

ROGER-VIOLLET/THE IMAGE WORKS

EVERETT

FRED W. MCDARRAH

Opposite, clockwise from top left: Blind Willie McTell, circa 1920; Danny and the Juniors on *American Bandstand* in 1958; Beat Generation writer Jack Kerouac in 1959; Buddy Holly in the mid-1950s; the 19th century French symbolist poet Arthur Rimbaud, who influenced 20th century artists from Picasso to Patti Smith, as well as Dylan. This page, clockwise from top left: Little Richard in the 1950s; Pete Seeger in 1964; Woody Guthrie in the postwar period; Hank Williams in the early 1950s.

Plugging In

- -

Dylan, even beyond his singular singing voice, was going to be difficult for lots of people. It is good to understand that this was an inevitability; he was simply a difficult guy when measured against standard norms of social or professional interaction.

"I wanted to meet the mind that created all those beautiful words," the singer Judy Collins told the author David Hajdu when he was assembling material for *Positively 4th Street*, his fine group portrait of Dylan and the Baez sisters, Joan and Mimi, and of Richard Fariña (who would become Mimi's husband) and other creatures of the Village in the early 1960s. "We set something up," continued Collins, "and we had coffee, and when it was over, I walked away, thinking, 'The guy's an idiot. He can't make a coherent sentence.'" Baez herself recalled for Hajdu the first time she ever heard Dylan sing, having previously met him: "I never thought something so powerful could come out of that little toad."

Yes, Dylan could be difficult to fathom or just plain difficult, even for those close to him. What can be seen as an inherent petulance both was and was not an act. Like his friend Allen Ginsberg, he enjoyed toying with his inquisitors: a cat pawing the mouse during any kind of Q&A. But this wasn't a habit he developed only after he was famous and was therefore in a position of power.

Consider an episode he recounts in *Chronicles: Volume One*. It's the fall of 1961, John Hammond has just signed him to a standard contract at Columbia Records and has handed him over to Billy James, the publicity chief of the label, who is "dressed Ivy League like" and whose job it is to put together the Dylan dossier for dissemination to the press.

Remember: Dylan is still a kid, a nobody, and hasn't recorded a single song.

James asks Dylan where he's from and Dylan says Illinois. "He asked me if I ever did any other work and I told him that I had a dozen jobs, drove a bakery truck once. He wrote that down and asked me if there was anything else. I said I'd worked construction and he asked me where.

"'Detroit.'

"'You traveled around?'

"'Yep.'

"He asked me about my family, where they were. I told him I had no idea, that they were long gone.

"'What was your home life like?'

"I told him I'd been kicked out."

It goes on like this with poor Mr. James for a while. "I hated these kind of questions," writes Dylan, who would hate them forever. "Felt I could ignore them."

- -

Can this cat prowling in London in 1966 possibly be the same one we saw pictured in New York on page nine? Those bright eyes are now hidden behind shades day and night, you could never stuff all that hair into one of those folkie caps, denims have yielded to leathers and the soft, open gaze has given way to an often brooding aspect. It can be said, however: The evolving image fits the changing music.

James asks him how he got to New York City. "I rode a freight train."

"'You mean a passenger train?'

"'No, a freight train.'

"'You mean, like a boxcar?'

"'Yeah, like a boxcar. Like a freight train.'

"'Okay, a freight train.'"

Again, remember: This is Dylan at his brand new—really, his first—place of employment. This is Dylan having just been handed his big break.

Finally, James asks Dylan whom he sees himself resembling in the contemporary music scene. "I told him, nobody. That part of things was true, I really didn't see myself like anybody. The rest of it, though, was pure hokum—hophead talk."

Dylan really *wasn't* like anyone else, and not only as pertains to his sound and songs. Call it truculence or integrity, but this fierce, immutable quirk in his personality allowed him to walk out on Ed Sullivan (Columbia Records must have been delighted about that); allowed him to treat Suze Rotolo cruelly at Newport in 1963 when introducing her to his new lover, Baez; allowed him to accept credit for what seemed, to many listeners, other people's arrangements; allowed him to cuff Billy James around when the guy was only doing his job; allowed him, through the decades, to phone in a good number of subpar concerts in addition to the sensational ones; and would allow him to go electric.

Chronicles: Volume One is a wonderful book, and a fascinating one. Dylan regularly recounts in its pages what might be considered by others to be embarrassing episodes, but there is very little or no remorse. The book is self-reflective, but it also has a *well, that's the way it is—that's the way I am* quality. Perhaps more to the point: *You go your way and I'll go mine.*

But, of course, Dylan intended (or, while never admitting it, *hoped*) that an audience would go his way too—following him, moths to the flame, because of his irresistible dynamism and obvious brilliance. "It wasn't money or love that I was looking for," he writes. "I had a heightened sense of awareness, was set in my ways, impractical and a visionary to boot. My mind was strong like a trap and I didn't need any guarantee of validity. I didn't know a single soul in this dark freezing metropolis but that was all about to change—and quick."

As we have already seen, it did change—very quickly indeed. Within a season, he became the folk darling of downtown. With Baez's considerable help, he went national not too very long after shaking the dust of Hibbing off his jeans.

And now, what next?

Albert Grossman is a very interesting player in this saga. A hard-charging Chicagoan who sidled into the folk scene and started managing individuals and group acts, he hit it big with the trio Peter, Paul and Mary (he was pivotal in assembling the threesome in 1961) and would go on to promote the careers of Gordon Lightfoot, Richie Havens, the Band and Janis Joplin among others. Dylan signed with him in 1962. In *Chronicles: Volume One* the singer has a marvelous reminiscence of watching Grossman as he was trolling for

Dylan has found that he likes life in Woodstock, New York, and that is where these pictures and the ones on the following pages were made in 1964. We have mentioned that Dylan was influenced by Jack Kerouac and the Beats; his direct association with that group was always through his friendship with poet Allen Ginsberg (opposite). On this page, at top, Dylan and fellow musician John Sebastian head out on a motorbike. Above: He would scribble lyrics any place, any time, and in the workroom he types them.

talent at the Gaslight, the Greenwich Village folk mecca: "He looked like Sidney [*sic*] Greenstreet from the film *The Maltese Falcon*, had an enormous presence, dressed always in a conventional suit and tie, and he sat at a corner table. Usually when he talked, his voice was loud, like the booming of war drums. He didn't talk so much as growl." Dylan signed with him in 1962, despite the fact that Grossman took 25 percent of earnings versus the standard manager's cut of 15 percent, Grossman's rationale being that a client became 10 percent smarter the minute he or she spoke with him. Dylan, as always, was savvy about what he was entering into; he saw Grossman's power and sway instantly. "He was kind of like a Colonel Tom Parker figure," he says in Martin Scorsese's *No Direction Home*, "you could smell him coming." In the same film, John Cohen, one of the New Lost City Ramblers and an accomplished photographer who, as an integral part of the scene, was making memorable photographs of Dylan and other folkies in the early '60s, says, "I don't think Albert manipulated Bob, because Bob was weirder than Albert."

Which took considerable weirdness, a quality Dylan always possessed in deep quantities. Dylan knew what he was getting with Grossman, and in a sense turned him loose: a hired gun. Grossman didn't like John Hammond, so halfway through *The Freewheelin' Bob Dylan* sessions, Hammond was replaced by the young African American producer Tom Wilson, who would help shepherd Dylan through four cuts on that record and then all of *The Times They Are A-Changin'*, *Another Side of Bob Dylan*, *Bringing It All Back Home* and the seminal 1965 track "Like a Rolling Stone," regarded by many, including the magazine that bears the same name, as the very greatest cut in rock history.

Skinny little Bob Dylan, with new friends like Joan Baez and Albert Grossman, was flexing his muscles. Grossman saw just how strong, determined and talented his new client was, and—no sweet-hearted Brian Epstein, he—started pushing people around in a manner not unlike that in which Dylan was manhandling the interviewers Grossman summoned forth. Perhaps the most famous example of the singer's own bad behavior remains Dylan's cruel taunting of a *Time* magazine London-based correspondent, Horace Freeland Judson, during the 1965 tour of England, an incident still remembered today because it was captured by documentarian D.A. Pennebaker's camera and was included in the terrific 1967 film *Dont Look Back*. Pennebaker, who was well inside the Dylan orbit, observed the singer's operation closely and with clear eyes, and later said of Grossman and his handling of the enterprise: "I think Albert was one of the few people that saw Dylan's worth very early on, and played it absolutely without equivocation or any kind of compromise."

In other words: The fans, the festivals, the press, the whole wide world could take Dylan on his and Albert Grossman's terms, or not at all.

- -

Above: Writer Mason Hoffenberg, John Sebastian and Dylan chat in a Woodstock cafe. In 1964, Sebastian is a year away from forming his own hit-making band, the Lovin' Spoonful, and is often hanging with Dylan. Opposite: Sebastian is playing acoustic guitar and Dylan is on a solid-body *electric* bass in the otherwise quiet cafe. Sebastian will take part in some of the sessions that produce *Bringing It All Back Home*.

Left: This photo made in Woodstock of Albert Grossman's wife, Sally, and Dylan will eventually grace the cover of *Bringing It All Back Home.* During sessions for that album and its 1965 companion, *Highway 61 Revisited,* Dylan tries out all sorts of things on all of his instruments—piano (below), harmonica, acoustic and electric guitars—in ways he hadn't earlier. Opposite: In Woodstock, Sara Lowndes watches films with Dylan and his friend Victor Maymudes in 1964. In this period she and Dylan are becoming romantically involved, and the next year she will become pregnant and they will wed. Maymudes, who died in 2001, was regarded on the scene as "the Village philosopher" and something of a mentor to Dylan; he served at various times through the years as the singer's tour manager.

PHOTOGRAPH © DANIEL KRAMER

MICHAEL OCHS ARCHIVES/GETTY

Dylan's musical terms, beginning in 1964 and continuing through the recording of *Bringing It All Back Home*'s electric sessions in 1965, were changing rapidly. Lyrically, he was moving away from narrative tales and so-called protest songs wherein the message was more or less directly stated; he was, in his writing, becoming more abstract, opaque, allusive. In some songs, he wrote in a stream of consciousness vein clearly influenced by Jack Kerouac and his Beat Generation confreres.

In the summer of '64 he spent much time out of the Greenwich Village orbit, staying often at Grossman's place in the small upstate hamlet of Woodstock, where he could think and compose. Among the things he was thinking about, in a positive way, was the electric blues sound his friend John Hammond Jr. was working on in Chicago. (Just incidentally, Hammond, who was the son of producer John Hammond, had recruited for that effort a group that included three musicians who would be members of Dylan's famous backing collaborative known first as the Hawks, later as the Band.) Dylan was restless with energy, recalled Joan Baez, who stayed with him that August at Grossman's Woodstock home: "Most of the month or so we were there, Bob stood at the typewriter in the corner of his room, drinking red wine and smoking and tapping away relentlessly for hours. And in the dead of night, he would wake up, grunt, grab a cigarette, and stumble over to the typewriter again." Late that month, Dylan traveled down to the city where he met the Beatles for the first time. The story is always told about how this summit influenced the Englishmen, who were turned on to marijuana by Dylan and subsequently began to look for a Dylanesque introspection and depth in their own compositions. But

perhaps the inspiration cut both ways, as Dylan was already thinking about electric music and rock 'n' roll, and now here were these super-popular moptops who were actually pretty fine fellows. (He and the Beatles would remain close; he and George Harrison would become something like best friends.)

A couple of the songs that would be featured on the largely acoustic Side Two of *Bringing It All Back Home*—"Gates of Eden," "Mr. Tambourine Man"—had already been written but hadn't made it onto *Another Side of Bob Dylan*. Now, on January 13, 1965, Dylan sat with Tom Wilson in Columbia's Studio A in New York City and worked on, among others, eight songs that would be presented to a rock band over the following two days, "She Belongs to Me," "Bob Dylan's 115th Dream" and "Love Minus Zero/No Limit" among them. On January 14, with no rehearsal, the band—three guitarists, including Dylan, a pianist, electric bass, drums—charged ahead. In only three and a half hours that afternoon, master takes of the three just mentioned songs plus "Subterranean Homesick Blues" and "Outlaw Blues" were waxed. Back in Studio A on the 15th, "Maggie's Farm," Dylan's kiss-off to his protest-song disciples, was achieved in one take to kick off another memorable, fast-moving session, "It's Alright, Ma (I'm Only Bleeding)," and "It's All Over Now, Baby Blue" being other classics addressed this day.

The album, which featured a cover photograph taken by Daniel Kramer at Grossman's Woodstock home, with Grossman's wife, Sally, lounging on a couch in the background, knocked people out, garnering Dylan thousands of new fans while alienating many old ones. "Subterranean Homesick Blues" became his first Top 40 hit in the United

Initially, some musical acts that might be called more "accessible" enjoyed bigger hits with Dylan's songs than he did. At left, Dylan is at Atlantic Studios in New York City with Sonny and Cher in 1965, and below he is onstage with the Byrds at Ciro's in L.A. that same year. (The Byrds, in particular, were regular Dylan interpreters.) Opposite: Country star Johnny Cash also sang Dylan compositions, and greatly boosted the younger man's credibility with a new crowd when he insisted that Dylan guest-star on the premiere episode of his new variety show. Cash made certain that Dylan did not have to show a passport to enter Nashville, nor steal in by dead of night.

by the high school principal back in Hibbing, but now he would. His recruited sidemen for the Newport gig were largely members of the Paul Butterfield Blues Band, including guitarist Mike Bloomfield. Dylan, who had performed three acoustic songs during a festival workshop earlier on July 24, apparently felt that Butterfield's band was being dissed by Newport organizers—organizers who had invited them in the first place. He said, in effect: If they think they can keep electric music off this stage, they can't. I'll show 'em. He quickly assembled a pickup band that not only included Bloomfield but another who had recently helped him record "Like a Rolling Stone," organist Al Kooper. In a marvelous clash of cultures, these ragtag renegades rehearsed that night in one of Newport's legendarily opulent mansions dating from America's Gilded Age.

On Sunday night, introduced by Peter Yarrow of Peter, Paul and Mary, Dylan, like Bloomfield, took the stage with a solid-body electric guitar, and the rumblings began not just onstage. When the band launched into "Maggie's Farm," the boos issued forth, and they continued, intermixed with competitive cheering, through "Like a Rolling Stone" and "Phantom Engineer," a prototype version of "It Takes a Lot to Laugh, It Takes a Train to Cry."

And then, that was it. Dylan and company left the stage, and the reaction was raucous. Yarrow begged him to return and Dylan did, but was upset. "What are you doing to me?" he asked Yarrow. He then asked the audience for a harmonica tuned in E, and a small shower of them pelted the stage. He performed, solo acoustic, "Mr. Tambourine Man" and "It's All Over Now, Baby Blue." Many in the audience who had missed the message of "Maggie's Farm" still missed it with this closing number, and the response this time was rapturous. Dylan, for his part, wouldn't return to Newport for 37 years.

There is a never-settled debate concerning the hostility exhibited at Newport: Was it largely due to a short set list, or

States and charted Top 10 in England, where the album went to Number One. (That single led to a pioneering music video when a sequence of Dylan tossing cue cards with lyrics from the song played during the opening of *Dont Look Back*; "Subterranean Homesick Blues" is also considered by some historians to be an early rap song.) Before Dylan ever took the stage as the headliner at Newport in the summer of '65, the "trad folkie" phase of his career was emphatically erstwhile, and the masses were chattering away, pro and con.

Dylan, now more famous than Baez, finished his most recent tour with her (he wouldn't collaborate with her onstage again until the Rolling Thunder Revue concerts a decade further on, an altered relationship largely of his choosing) and made plans for his new live act. He hadn't played an electric set since his r'n'r band had been silenced

to poor sound quality, or to the material ("tenth-rate drivel," according to folksinger Ewan MacColl), or to the fact of electric music? Dylan surely bought into the final reason, and felt he had been betrayed by old friends and fans. Four days after returning to New York from Newport, he recorded "Positively 4th Street," which seemed to promise that he would get his revenge on his former fellow travelers in the Village. If they wanted to see the future—at least, Dylan's future—they only needed to consider that "Like a Rolling Stone," a groundbreaking six-minute rock single, was at Number Two on the Billboard chart and was shaping the sound of a summer every bit as much as were the songs of Motown, the Beatles, the Stones and the Beach Boys. If it sold a couple fewer copies than the Kingsmen's "Jolly Green Giant" by the time the year was out, and if that was folkdom's rebuttal, well, so be it.

Not all of the old crowd deserted him. The late and great Dave Van Ronk, who always saw Dylan clearly even when he had cause to detest him for his aberrant and even unethical behavior, wrote in his posthumously published memoir: "I thought that going electric was a logical direction for Bobby to take. I did not care for all his new stuff, by any means, but some of it was excellent, and it was a reasonable extension of what he had done up to that point. And I knew perfectly well that none of us was a true 'folk' artist. We were professional performers, and while we liked a lot of folk music, we all liked a lot of other things as well. Working musicians are very rarely purists. The purists are out in the audience kibitzing, not onstage trying to make a living. And Bobby was absolutely right to ignore them."

The latter half of 1965 was no less eventful than the first. In confirmation of Side One of *Bringing It All Back Home* came the album *Highway 61 Revisited*, with Bloomfield, Kooper and other rockers along for the ride, and the songs even more out there—the 11-minute "Desolation Row" but one example. Dylan was going to appear in support of the record and his new sound, and needed to cobble together a band. From the *Highway 61* and "Like a Rolling Stone" sessions, he brought Kooper and bassist Harvey Brooks, adding to them members of that bar band called the Hawks—the same band John Hammond Jr. had been gigging with—the guitarist Robbie Robertson and the drummer Levon Helm. He warned his associates before taking the stage at the Forest Hills Tennis Stadium on August 28 that the reaction might be less than friendly. Daniel Kramer, who was there, later remembered: "Dylan held a conference with the musicians who were going

Two more photos from 1965. In the one below, Dylan displays cards with lyrics from "Subterranean Homesick Blues" for the camera of D.A. Pennebaker, who is filming what will become the opening sequence of his documentary *Dont Look Back*. Opposite: Peter Yarrow, Dylan and John Hammond Jr. hail a cab in New York.

- -

to accompany him in the second half of the concert. He told them they should expect anything to happen—he probably was remembering what occurred at Newport. He told them that the audience might yell and boo, and that they should not be bothered by it. Their job was to make the best music they were capable of, and let whatever happened happen."

It happened, pretty much as it had at Newport. A contemporaneous report from *Variety:* "Bob Dylan split 15,000 of his fans down the middle at Forest Hills Tennis Stadium Sunday night . . . The most influential writer-performer on the pop music scene during the past decade, Dylan has apparently evolved too fast for some of his young followers, who are ready for radical changes in practically everything else . . . repeating the same scene that occurred during his performance at the Newport Folk Festival, Dylan delivered a round of folk-rock songs but had to pound his material against a hostile wall of anti-claquers, some of whom berated him for betraying the cause of folk music."

Six days after the New York show, the reception was somewhat warmer out in laid back La La Land during a concert at the Hollywood Bowl, but the next year in England, now playing with four-fifths of what would become the Band (Levon Helm stayed home), hostility raised its head night after night. It was almost as if Dylan were courting complaint and controversy. Rather than just play an electric tour, where presumably the fans would know what they were paying for and could either show up or not, he repeated this format of opening the show with a folk guitar and harmonica, then switching to the

rock-band numbers just as soon as he had the older fans swaying and smiling blissfully. Was he trying to upset them? Well, this was Bob Dylan, wasn't it? This push-and-pull—this teasing and taunting, this pleasing the audience and then pissing it off—would reach a legendary (not to say, biblical) climax on May 17, 1966, late during a concert at the Free Trade Hall in Manchester, England.

A man in the audience shouts to the stage, "Judas!"

"I don't believe you," Dylan responds. "You're a liar!"

He then turns to his band, which is set to roar into "Like a Rolling Stone," and orders: "Play it [expletive] loud!"

So in Dylan's professional life, all is tempest, all is Sturm und Drang. In his personal life, post-Baez in late 1964 through 1965, all is bliss. Or a Dylan version of bliss.

He had first met the former Shirley Marlin Noznisky—born on October 28, 1939, in Delaware—in 1962, when, according to her family's lore, she had been driving in Greenwich Village in her MG. She was, at the time, Sara Lowndes, married to magazine photographer Hans Lowndes (who had asked her to change her first name as well as her second: "I can't be married to a woman named Shirley.") Sara was a New York City career girl of a certain type: fashion model, stage actress when

she could get a role, Playboy bunny when she needed a job. Her former stepson, Peter Lowndes, once said, "Her meeting with Bob was the reason [Sara left Hans Lowndes]—he was famous, and she was very beautiful."

If she separated from Lowndes soon after meeting Dylan, she and the singer would not become a couple for a while more—and not until Dylan had progressed through his relationships with Suze Rotolo and Baez. When, in late 1964, Dylan and Sara did get serious, they took apartments in the storied Chelsea Hotel in New York City to be near one another. By 1965, Bobby and Sara were living together in a

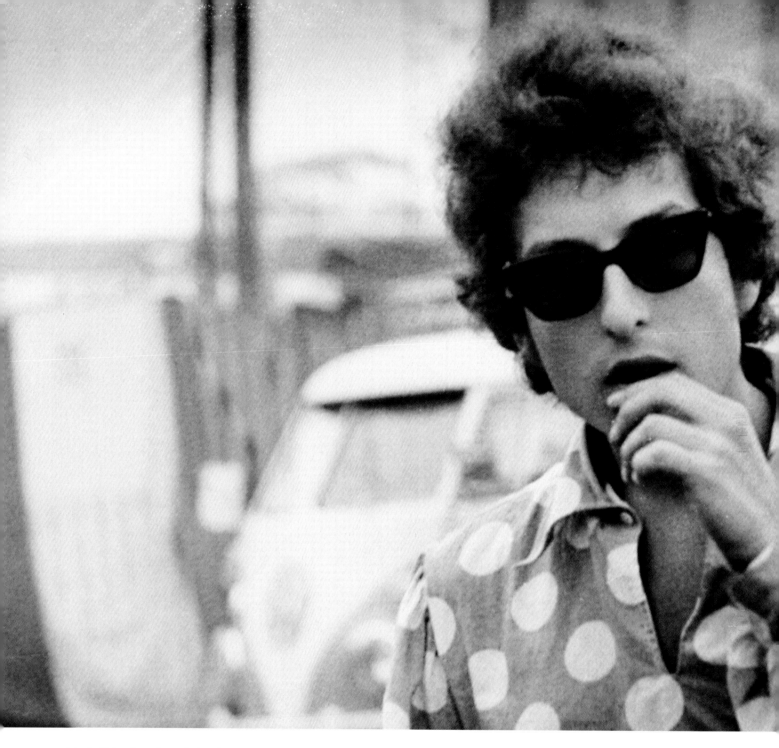

cabin in Woodstock, and that living was easy. He wrote "Like a Rolling Stone" in a heartbeat there: "It just came, you know."

Not long after the Hollywood Bowl concert, Dylan and Sara wed, on November 22, 1965, in a civil ceremony that was small and secret. (Dylan lied for a time to even close friends about having married, and it fell to Nora Ephron to make the news public the following February in a *New York Post* story headlined, HUSH! BOB DYLAN IS WED.) Exchanging vows in Mineola, Long Island, Dylan had only Albert Grossman in his wedding party and Sara had only her maid of honor.

Sara was content to suppress her ego in deference to her star husband and his career—she had little in common, in this vein, with Linda McCartney, Pattie Boyd or Yoko Ono—but

she was sometimes involved. She had already been instrumental before their marriage, for instance, in the Pennebaker documentary *Dont Look Back*. In fact, Pennebaker told biographer Robert Shelton, "The idea of the film was from his wife." Sara, after bringing Pennebaker in contact with Dylan and Grossman, continued to serve as a liaison on that production. But mostly, when it came to Dylan's music, Sara served as muse. She was, in 1966, the "Sad-Eyed Lady of the Lowlands," a song Dylan once told Shelton he considered perhaps his best. A decade later, in a plea for reconciliation after their marriage had failed, she was overtly the "Sara" on the *Desire* album. Those things we know for sure. It has also been speculated that Sara was at the heart of such songs

During a final sound check at Newport on July 25, 1965, Dylan wore a polka dot shirt, and the photographer Dick Waterman recently recalled to LIFE that the singer stopped and let Dick make this picture, then went off to change his clothes for the big show. So at the very moment registered here, Dylan knows full well what he is about to do, and perhaps what the reaction will be. Below, he does it, wielding his Fender Stratocaster like a sword as he duels with the crowd. Dylan has been investigating this new course for several months, of course, but now the course is firmly set.

as "Isis," "We Better Talk This Over," "Abandoned Love," "Down Along the Cove," "Wedding Song," "On a Night Like This," "Something There Is About You," "I'll Be Your Baby Tonight," "To Be Alone with You," "If Not for You," and those classics from the 1965 output: "Desolation Row" and "Love Minus Zero/No Limit." If the consensus opinion that 1975's *Blood on the Tracks*, with its recurring themes of loss, heartache and anger, represents perhaps the greatest breakup album of all time—an opinion Dylan refutes, insisting the songs were inspired by Chekhov short stories—then Sara's legacy extends. Jakob Dylan, the singer, dismisses his dad's demurral, asserting at one point to *The New York Times*, "When I'm listening to 'Subterranean Homesick Blues,' I'm

grooving along just like you. But when I'm listening to *Blood on the Tracks*, that's about my parents."

In the 10 years between the romance of *Bringing It All Back Home* and the recrimination of *Blood on the Tracks*, the Dylans lived in Woodstock—also back in New York City, out in Malibu, but often in Woodstock—and raised a family that would come to include their own four children, Jesse, Anna, Samuel and Jakob, plus Sara's daughter from her marriage to Lowndes, Maria, whom Dylan adopted. When at home, Dylan tried to live a sheltered existence, and Sara—as said, a rarity among rock star wives—stayed thoroughly out of the public eye. Still today, after so much effort has been put into unearthing Dylaniana through the decades, relatively little is

So Dylan has famously gone electric, and he is taking his show on the road. It's fabulous—it's *fab*—to compare the Dylan-invading-Europe photographs with pictures of the Beatles in America from the same approximate time. With the Englishmen, even though George Harrison in particular had already begun to hate the tours and they would soon end, the "lads" are still all smiles. Dylan obviously feels no such compunction. Maybe the booing is playing a part.

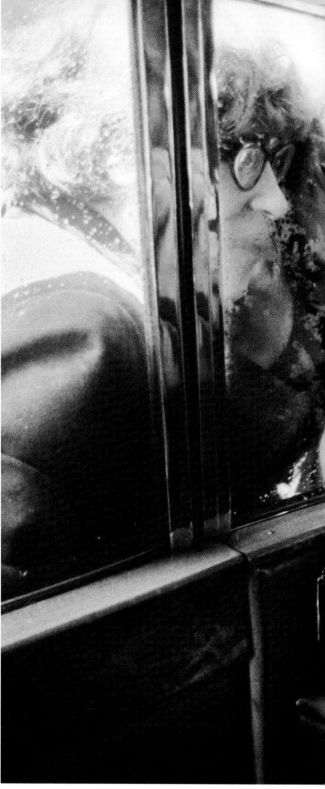

known about Sara. In the song that bears her name, Dylan calls her "radiant jewel, mystical wife," and there is certainly something of the spiritual to her image. It has been said that Dylan relied on her for the kind of guidance one might seek from an occultist; Sara would suggest when it was propitious to travel, and when it wasn't. Lynn Musgrave was a music journalist living in Woodstock, and knew Sara. She told Shelton, "She is not Mother Earth in the heavy way, but she just rolls with nature. She has a low center of gravity, if not

quite indestructible, then something close to it. That is what it must take to sit up there in Woodstock, being married to Dylan and never going out much. I don't think she complains much, either. I got the impression of her being strong. That line, 'she speaks like silence'—that's Sara." Shelton himself met Sara in 1968 at the first public function she attended with her famous husband, a tribute to Woody Guthrie at Carnegie Hall, and later wrote, "mostly on her own, [she] moved about rather shyly, gravitating toward people she knew from

Woodstock. She appeared demure, yet slightly ill at ease in a throng fascinated by her husband. I chatted briefly with her, and noted the deep large eyes, the glowing complexion, the air of quiet detachment. Friends of Sara considered her then as extremely warm and devoted toward a select few."

Her devotion to Dylan lasted until the mid-1970s and was followed by a bitter divorce, not finalized until 1977. To deal with all that now would be getting ahead of ourselves; that is material for the next chapter, and the one beyond that. Right now, we are still with the happily newlywed Dylans, 1965 is giving way to a new year, Dylan is determined to push his new sound upon his audience, and there is a new album coming out.

If *The Freewheelin' Bob Dylan, The Times They Are A-Changin'* and *Another Side of Bob Dylan* represented the artist's first great triptych—and if *Time Out of Mind, Love and Theft* and *Modern Times* represent a recent one—then Dylan's second group of three sibling albums, each of them a peak in his considerable creative output and featuring the "wild, mercury sound"

Dylan's 1966 World Tour is aggressive (left, in Paris on May 24, where Dylan addresses his hecklers: "Don't worry, I'm just as eager to finish and leave as you are"). And it is exhausting, as many of these subsequent photographs on the following five pages, all taken during the European leg of the road show, clearly imply. Kicking off in Louisville on February 4 and with more than half of its eventual 44 concerts in the U.S. and Canada, the tour travels to Australia (seven shows in 14 days), Sweden, Denmark, Ireland, Wales, England, Scotland, France and then back to London for the grand finale at the Royal Albert Hall (opposite, at the sound check there). It closes up shop on May 27, and Dylan and friends flee for home.

that was then his quest, comprised *Bringing It All Back Home*, *Highway 61 Revisited* and *Blonde on Blonde*. This last one, an unprecedented double-album set that included "Sad-Eyed Lady of the Lowlands" as the entirety of Side Four, also gave the world "Rainy Day Women #12 & 35," "I Want You," "Just Like a Woman," "Visions of Johanna" (an eternal masterpiece, which Dylan wrote while living in the Chelsea Hotel with his pregnant wife) and several others. It was recorded in Nashville with seasoned musicians, after Dylan, Robbie Robertson and Al Kooper had arrived from New York with this bushel of new songs. *Blonde on Blonde* pushed the music further, and now folk, rock and country, too, were all in the mix.

By the time it was released in the spring of 1966, Dylan and his backing band the Hawks were in Australia being chided and derided on a daily basis in the press and on a nightly basis in the auditorium. Dylan was wearing those Beatle boots, shirts as outrageous as his hair and 24/7 sunglasses. He was also not responding well to the pressure and venom and was, according to D.A. Pennebaker, who was still hanging around with his camera, "taking a lot of amphetamine and who-knows-what-else."

"I was on drugs, a lot of things," Dylan later admitted to *Rolling Stone*'s Jann Wenner, "just to keep going, you know? . . . I was on the road for almost five years. It wore me down." But he persevered, moving through Europe and toward England.

It's interesting: Judged not by total sales but by chart position, Dylan's early folk records had been more popular in Great Britain than in his homeland, even though many of his topical songs were directed at life in the United States. The acoustic Dylan was a god to British folkies, and his 1965 tour had been an unequivocal triumph. Now came this wise-guy, would-be rocker—a Mick Jagger manqué who couldn't pull it off, and who refused to sing what the audience wanted, refused to explain himself and refused to give anyone a straight

answer to anything. His February 1966 interview in *Playboy*, conducted more or less cordially by the respected music writer Nat Hentoff, remains the classic of its kind mostly because Hentoff decided early (and wisely) to play the straight man, and allow Dylan to entertain in his way. Dialogue taken verbatim from this interview was used as the absurdist lines voiced by Cate Blanchett in the acclaimed 2007 filmic Dylan rumination by Todd Haynes, *I'm Not There*. A representative exchange from the original interview:

PLAYBOY: Mistake or not, what made you decide to go the rock 'n' roll route?

DYLAN: Carelessness. I lost my one true love. I started drinking. The first thing I know, I'm in a card game. Then I'm in a crap game. I wake up in a pool hall. Then this big Mexican lady drags me off the table, takes me to Philadelphia. She leaves me alone in her house, and it burns down. I wind up in Phoenix. I get a job as a Chinaman. I start working in a dime store, and move in with a 13-year-old girl. Then this big Mexican lady from Philadelphia comes in and burns the house down. I go down to Dallas. I get a job as a "before" in a Charles Atlas "before and after" ad. I move in with a delivery boy who can cook fantastic chili and hot dogs. Then this 13-year-old girl from Phoenix comes and burns the house down. The delivery boy—he ain't so mild: He gives her the knife, and the next thing I know I'm in Omaha. It's so cold there, by this time I'm robbing my own bicycles and frying my own fish. I stumble onto some luck and get a job as a carburetor out at the hot-rod races every Thursday night. I move in with a high school teacher who also does a little plumbing on the side, who ain't much to look at, but who's built a special kind of refrigerator that can turn newspaper into lettuce. Everything's going good until that delivery boy shows up and

Left: As Dylan breaks bread in Birmingham, England, with his backing musicians, the Hawks—most of whom eventually will become better known as the Band—the feeling at the table might well be what this tableau so resembles: a last supper. Certainly there are laughs behind the scenes (below, with friend Bob Neuwirth), but just as often there are whispered strategy sessions with manager Albert Grossman (opposite). Everyone is trying to cope with something that is unspooling not quite as hoped. And yet night after night, as Robbie Robertson of the Band attests, the music is getting better and better. The tour will end—and there will not be another one for nearly eight years—but this new sound will live on.

----

followed went well, the "Judas" allegation in Manchester being only the most enduring moment. The Royal Albert Hall shows in London were perhaps the most dispiriting. Dylan mixed it up with his accusers, seldom a sound strategy for rapprochement, and the situation devolved, with the Beatles at one point shouting from their box to others in the audience, "Leave him alone—*shut up!*"

tries to knife me. Needless to say, he burned the house down, and I hit the road. The first guy that picked me up asked me if I wanted to be a star. What could I say?

And the interview went on and on in this vein, concluding with:

PLAYBOY: One final question: Even though you've more or less retired from political and social protest, can you conceive of any circumstance that might persuade you to reinvolve yourself?

DYLAN: No, not unless all the people in the world disappeared.

Playboy magazine was, even back in the day, able to cross the Atlantic—the British said they liked it for the articles, essays and short stories—and by the time Dylan stepped foot in the kingdom on this tour, Newport and *Playboy* were both on the table, and the knives were out. None of what

In May 1966, Dylan and the Hawks returned to America, beaten if not quite broken. All Dylan wanted was rest, a slower speed. Woodstock looked, in his imagining, to be the answer for the next little while—Sara, the baby, et cetera. But he soon learned that Woodstock, and whatever it represented in his mind, would have to wait. ABC was eager for a documentary film of the world tour that had been contracted earlier. The Macmillan publishing firm was pointing to a deadline for an agreed-upon book (which would end up being the narrative poem *Tarantula*). Grossman handed Dylan an itinerary of tour dates that he had set up for the rest of the summer, extending into autumn.

The late Robert Shelton, a journalist who made the journalist's mistake of growing too close to his subject, remembered in his 1986 book, *No Direction Home:* "Late Friday night, July 29, I received a telephone call from Hibbing. Dylan's father sounded distraught: 'They just called me from the radio station here. They said they had a news bulletin that Bob's been badly hurt in a motorcycle accident. Do you know anything about it?' I said this was the first I had heard of it.

'The Grossman office won't help me one bit on this,' said Abe. 'And I can't get through to Sara. Would you please see if you can find out something—anything—and call us back, collect? Bob's mother is very worried—and so am I.' Four months earlier, a similar phone call had informed me of [folksinger Richard] Fariña's death in a motorcycle accident. I rang *The New York Times* for more information." Shelton soon learned: "Details about Dylan's accident . . . were not easy to ascertain. It was widely reported that Dylan nearly lost his life. To me, it seems more likely that his mishap *saved* his life. The locking of the back wheel of Dylan's Triumph 500 started a chain of redemptive events that allowed him to slow down."

No ambulance had been called to the scene; Dylan hadn't been admitted to any hospital. Dylan has said that he broke several vertebrae in the crash, but there is no injury report. What happened?

The suggestion has been made that Dylan, faced with unrelenting pressure of his own initial making, panicked, and perhaps spun out with something approaching purposefulness. Dylan, for once, will not argue the point, and has written in *Chronicles: Volume One*—which is as elliptical as it wants to be, when it wants to be—"I had been in a motorcycle accident and I'd been hurt, but I recovered. Truth was I wanted to get out of the rat race."

He convalesced in Woodstock.

He ate better, and dressed more casually.

He and Sara continued to build their family.

He would occasionally turn up for a benefit concert or surprise appearance, but essentially he retired from the stage for most of the next decade.

He found it more difficult to write songs.

He thought about becoming more serious about his painting.

If he wondered what the future of Bob Dylan might be, well, to this day he still hasn't admitted to that.

In *Chronicles: Volume One*, Dylan, who is never one to wave a white flag, freely admits that he required something new after the battering of the world tour— he needed, in as much of a concession as he will ever make, to get out of what he called "the rat race." What had happened: The wave of criticism, which barely existed in America in February, had built as the tour progressed, until the point where it became truly ugly in England: nightly walkouts, epithets screamed, a savage press corps. In a remarkable and unfortunate way, this major rock 'n' roll tour began to feel like anything but: no rapturous welcomes, no fifth encores, no partying after the concert. "After those shows we were lonely guys," Robbie Robertson remembered later. "Nobody wanted to hang out with us." When it was finally over, Dylan knew there were a few folks somewhere whom he was eager to hang out with: his family, in Woodstock. He was eager to get home.

Dylan and the Band

Mostly Canadian by birth—Robbie Robertson, Rick Danko, Garth Hudson and Richard Manuel were all from north of the border, while Levon Helm hailed from Arkansas—their sound was a blend of Americana and roadhouse rock 'n' roll. They weren't Dylan's first electric backing band, nor his last, but they were with him in Woodstock, and at the Royal Albert Hall (minus Helm). They shared the catcalls and, later, the cheers.

MICHAEL OCHS ARCHIVES/GETTY

KEN REGAN/CAMERA 5

JAN PERSSON/REDFERNS/GETTY

Opposite, clockwise from top left: One iteration of the Hawks in the early 1960s (the two guys at left wouldn't make the journey toward becoming the Band); Dylan, backed by the boys, at Carnegie Hall in 1968; touring America in 1974; Dylan, with Richard Manuel, in the shades that he hid behind as England booed in 1966. This page, bottom left: Dylan, Danko and Helm in 1983. In the photo just below, made in Woodstock in 1968, the guys seem almost to be posing for the group portrait painted by Dylan, which served as the cover art of their landmark debut album, *Music from Big Pink* (bottom right).

ELLIOTT LANDY/CORBIS

KEN REGAN/CAMERA 5

LYNN GOLDSMITH/CORBIS

COURTESY BUD KLIMENT

Retreat, Return

Dylan wanted to get out of the rat race, sure, and whether he purposely caused his exit from the scene or it was forced upon him, there was an irony to the first weeks and months of his rehabilitation—physical, psychological, spiritual rehab—in Woodstock. The irony: Nothing was calm, all was chaos. If anything, it was even worse than it had recently been. Dylan's fans desperately wanted to know how he was and what had happened. Journalists were their only agents, and so the drumbeat from the press was ceaseless. Across the globe a story ran in a Japanese newspaper recounting a bedside interview in a hospital— an interview that had never happened. It was all so very ponderous and urgent, as Dylan lay at home rubbing his neck. This, from the respectable *Chicago Tribune:* "A traditional gesture of the prophet is the retreat and the re-emergence . . . with a new message. A good deal of what will or won't be in pop music hangs on Dylan's re-emergence and his message." Prophet, please, re-emerge!

The temptation with Dylan is to assume he was amused, but he wasn't, not at this juncture. He was surely worried. Albert Grossman was out there downplaying the seriousness of his client's injuries and insisting Dylan would be back at work—meaning, back on the road—in a matter of weeks. (Meanwhile, Grossman was fuming as he stomped around the office, "How could he do this to me?") Dylan was insisting, because he felt compelled to, that he had indeed been hurt, and might not return to touring or even recording anytime soon. When Robert Shelton speculated in *The New York Times* that the injuries might not be as critical as previously thought, Dylan's brother, David, quickly departed the singer's camp in Woodstock to quell this most injurious of speculations. He traveled to the city and told Shelton directly, "There *was* an accident. There definitely *was* an accident."

Shelton continued in his Dylan biography with a paragraph that seems to completely delineate what was going on,

and how, even if Dylan hadn't caused the crash, he somehow welcomed it: "Dylan only told me, 'It happened one morning after I'd been up for three days. I hit an oil slick. The weather still affects the wound.' He said he was riding along Striebel Road, not far from his Woodstock home, taking the bike into the garage for repairs, when the back wheel locked and he went hurtling over the handlebars. After the fall, he was rushed in a friend's car [to his doctor in nearby Middletown] with reported broken vertebrae of the neck, a possible concussion, and head and facial bruises. A major concert at the

Back in Woodstock, the beards would come and go, the shades would come and go, the cigarettes would come and go, the hair would get shorter and longer. The music would be made more intermittently, as the frantic rush of the young Bob Dylan was curtailed by circumstance. This proved to be a good thing.

Yale Bowl, scheduled for eight days later, was canceled. Dylan only knows just how severely he was hurt and at what point in his convalescence he discovered that he wanted to think, reorganize his life, spend time with his family, and listen to the silence." Even if it was as bad as reported, the accident became a metaphor, a time for change, a possibility of release, the start of seven and a half years of withdrawal to a more tranquil existence.

All these decades later, we can imagine Albert Grossman spinning in his grave.

Over time, the storm passed, and Dylan was, if never forgotten, at least back-burnered. He certainly had work to engage him—"new priorities," as he put it—in fatherhood. Jesse Byron Dylan was born on January 6, 1966 (he would grow to be a businessman and filmmaker; in 2008 he directed will.i.am in an Emmy-winning music video *Yes We Can* that supported Barack Obama's quest for the White House), and Anna Leigh Dylan arrived on July 11, 1967 (she is today an artist based in Santa Monica, California). Sara would give birth to Samuel Isaac Abraham Dylan and Jakob Luke Dylan in the next two years, completing the family as it would be constituted in Woodstock. A person might ordinarily suppose that Dylan was an absent parent—busy and peripatetic as he had been his whole life, constitutionally eccentric as he was—but the children certainly benefitted from Dad's extended downtime in the late 1960s and early '70s. He was often home, driving the station wagon, singing lullabies and even, if we can guess from the ear-and-mind-boggling 2009 album *Christmas in the Heart*, holiday carols. The idea of the nuclear Dylans sitting close to the hearth in Woodstock and harmonizing on "O Little Town of Bethlehem" or "Must Be Santa" brings great cheer.

When Dylan began to work again, he did so from home. One project he became deeply involved with was the editing of the Pennebaker footage from the 1966 tour, which was intended to become a follow-up film to *Dont Look Back* and air as part of ABC television's *Stage '66* series. Pennebaker later said that Dylan essentially commandeered the film. Whatever, the rough cut that was shown to ABC was rejected as far too bizarre for a national audience. The film did get finished— sort of—and today exists as the never commercially released and seldom screened *Eat the Document* (a double bill of this and *Renaldo and Clara*—we'll get to that—might be seen as Dylan waterboarding). As with anything Dylan, there were vignettes, outtakes and side-stories that today not only fascinate in memory but actually can be accessed. Martin Scorsese used bits of *Eat the Document* in *No Direction Home*. A duet of Dylan and Johnny Cash performing "I Still Miss Someone" is charming. Cut from the documentary (perhaps by Dylan himself) but available on bootleg versions is an extended scene of John Lennon (of all people!) counseling an addled, exhausted Dylan during a limo ride: "Come, come, boy, it's only a film. Pull yourself together." Lennon later told *Rolling Stone* that he and Dylan had both been on "junk," and later still, the Lennon-Dylan car ride provided fodder, as did the

Nat Hentoff *Playboy* interview, for Cate Blanchett's scenes in the film *I'm Not There*. Very little in the Dylan universe goes wasted—or, in any event, unseen.

Why Dylan, in the serenity of Woodstock, would want to spend his time revisiting the madness of the disastrous '66 world tour is anyone's guess. Far closer to what he was trying to accomplish in his psychic recovery was his measured, if purposeful, return to music-making. According to Shelton, Dylan was insistent at this time that "there must be another way of life for the pop star, in which *he* is in control, not *they*. He had to find ways of working to his own advantage with the recording industry, his book publisher, the TV network. He had to come to terms with his one-time friend, longtime manager, parttime neighbor, and sometime landlord, Albert Grossman." This he would do, but not quite yet; he and Grossman would

Bob and Sara and Anna are on the porch of their Byrdcliffe home in 1968, and then Bob is in the living room with Jesse and Maria, his adopted daughter, the same year. The Byrdcliffe Arts Colony is interesting. A utopian/artistic community just outside Woodstock, 1,500 bucolic acres nestled in the foothills of the Catskill Mountains and facing Mount Guardian, it was founded in 1902. Over time, it did not succeed, and eventually some land and properties were put up for sale. Because of the spirit of the place, artsy types were attracted. Dylan and his family lived in a house there, on Ohayo Mountain Road, in the 1960s and early '70s.

not part ways until 1970. But a first step in redefining life for this pop star was to just sing and play, quietly, with friends, and without an agenda.

The therapeutic new music-making we speak of, which really was done without an eye to any commercial potential, involved the men who had, in recent months, dared to take the stage with him night after night and face the catcalls, the boo-birds and the occasional thrown object. The musicians who were about to morph from the Hawks into the Band needed a bit of quietude just as much as Dylan did, and one by one they drifted into Woodstock—to see what the boss was up to, and to see what might be next for themselves.

One reason, certainly, that the Band relocated is that Dylan had put each of them on a weekly retainer—Rick Danko and Richard Manuel, as if "working," started visiting Dylan regularly to help with *Eat the Document*. But an even larger reason was that they had realized, by the time the previous year's tour had hit England, that they and Dylan had discovered what Robbie Robertson called "this thing": this terrific sound that was unlike any prior Dylan sound and very much unlike that of the roadhouse Hawks. The audiences hadn't heard it—they were too busy screaming bloody murder—but the guys onstage certainly had. It was worth exploring further.

Danko and Manuel very much liked the Woodstock vibe, and as Danko recalled later, "The next I knew, I found that big pink house that was in the middle of a hundred acres with a pond [in neighboring West Saugerties]. It was nice." Garth Hudson moved in with his bandmates Manuel and Danko, and Robertson and his future wife, Dominique, took a place nearby. If this period of Dylan and the Band's rocking-and-rolling life is preserved in the minds of their fans as some kind of up-country idyll, well, that's fine—it actually was that. Robertson said later that everyone remembers the period with great affection, that it marked the first time since they were kids that they hadn't been heading to a gig somewhere. Danko chimed in, "It was sure nice to have that time where

All photographs from 1968: Bob and Sara, with Jesse, Anna and Sam, at home in Byrdcliffe; Jesse and Bob outside the home; Bob doing his truck-and-guitar thing, perhaps thinking of Woody. It's certainly not all an act: After the motorcycle accident, he really was doing a truck-and-guitar thing, driving *"keep-'em-running"* vehicles every day and regaining his musical footing with the help of his friends in the Band. Once Sara asked him and the boys to rehearse elsewhere, the family station wagon became his conveyance to Danko's big pink house, where some of the most memorable American music ever made was miraculously captured on tape.

ELLIOTT LANDY/MAGNUM (3)

It is known that Dylan sometimes sneaks back into Hibbing, Minnesota, unannounced. He doesn't necessarily hold court at Zimmy's, the local bar and grill upon whose walls some of the rare photographs seen in this book hang, but he does go back on occasion. It is certain he remembers as well the times with friends and his kid down at the bakery in Woodstock, before crazies from all over the world found him—and drove him out.

we weren't under the pressures of the public, to be able to afford the time and place to do our homework, to reflect and push forward. It was a great time in life. It was just us getting together every day and playing homemade music."

"It was relaxed and low-key, which was something we hadn't enjoyed since we were children," said Hudson. "We could wander off into the woods with Hamlet"—the big dog that the Hawks shared with Dylan—"the woods were right outside our door."

In the spring of '67, Dylan and his four friends, who still saw themselves as the Hawks but considered their band very much on hiatus (Levon Helm hadn't even shown up yet), started informal recording sessions at Dylan's house, Hi Lo Ha. But there was the baby there, Jesse, who needed his naps, and so the gang relocated to the basement of Danko's digs, nicknamed Big Pink. Hudson cobbled together the recording equipment—a tape recorder and mixers borrowed from Grossman, microphones borrowed from Peter, Paul and

Mary—and what would become known as *The Basement Tapes* began. "That's really the way to do a recording," Dylan later told Jann Wenner, "in a peaceful, relaxed setting—in somebody's basement. With the windows open . . . and a dog lying on the floor."

In keeping with that ethos, Dylan brought to the proceedings sheaves of old-to-ancient material: traditional songs, folk songs, murder ballads. "It wasn't the train we came in on," said Robertson, who added that the first several weeks were spent just "killing time." But then the sound that had been achieved on tour, imbued now with this Americana, started to become its own thing, and Dylan began writing, often in collaboration with the others. "I Shall Be Released" came forth, as did "This Wheel's on Fire," "Quinn the Eskimo (The Mighty Quinn)" and "You Ain't Goin' Nowhere." Richard Manuel, who would succumb to addictions and died in a suicide in 1986, once remembered how casual and giddy and fantastically productive the creative process was at Big Pink: Dylan "came down to the basement with a piece of typewritten paper . . . and he said, 'Have you got any music for this?' . . . I had a couple of musical movements that fit . . . so I just elaborated a bit, because I wasn't sure what the lyrics meant. I couldn't run upstairs and say, What's this mean, Bob? 'Now the heart is filled with gold as if it was a purse.'" Dylan/Band aficionados have already registered: The song became "Tears of Rage."

Dylan recorded more than 100 songs and perhaps 30 new compositions in the basement, with himself and the others huddled near their mikes and playing temperately so that the sound wouldn't distort off the cement walls and so that the vocals could be heard. Helm showed up finally, and the Band, sans their master but having learned valuable lessons in songwriting, recorded early versions of the songs that would anchor their classic first album, *Music from Big Pink.* Elsewhere in this approximate period—the heady mid-1960s—in far more luxe environs, the Beatles and Beach Boys were finishing work on *Sgt. Pepper's Lonely Hearts Club Band* and *Pet Sounds:* great, intricately produced albums. This material from Big Pink was music of another sort, and it wasn't at all clear that it would ever make it up from the cellar. The bootleg history of these sessions and their eventual authorized release as *The Basement Tapes* is hardly worth recounting; some of the lore and legend has been beaten to a place beyond death. The larger point is: In the mid-1960s, giants of the decade—John Lennon, Paul McCartney, Brian Wilson, Bob Dylan—were at work in vastly different ways in studios in London, L.A. and a pink-painted house in upstate New York. They were making music that would endure, and which of it proves most enduring will be interesting to investigate a hundred years further on.

At the time, of course, the Big Pink sessions meant little to Dylan besides the fact that they were fun and fruitful, and he was able to bond with the guys and with the dog. The daily jamming represented a distinct break from what he had been up to just before the motorcycle accident. No one

was booing. Those sessions were good in and of themselves, just for these little mercies. They were revivifying.

In retrospect, it seems that, following the making of *Blonde on Blonde* and now the quieter life in laid-back Woodstock, it was natural for Dylan to return to Nashville—that place, that pace, that sound. He did so, and produced back-to-back country albums, *John Wesley Harding* and *Nashville Skyline*. But they were different from each other, and the difference is worth noting. *John Wesley Harding* is a tremendous record.

Dylan's father had died from a heart attack, Dylan had gone home for the funeral, Sara had given birth to the couple's third child, Dylan was about to re-emerge from the seclusion that followed his accident. There was nearly as much pressure on him now as there had been before the accident, and in a deliberate way, he responded brilliantly. *John Wesley Harding* bestowed the world with "All Along the Watchtower," and that would have been quite enough, but there was more: "The Wicked Messenger," "I'll Be Your Baby Tonight" and others.

Think of Big Pink as the Sun Studios of the Catskills. Really: *The Basement Tapes* is similar to Elvis Presley's seminal *Sun Sessions* in several ways. Here was a preternaturally gifted American artist playing passionately but off the cuff with his good friends—maybe his strongest collaborators ever?—without, necessarily, great expectations. (Okay, Elvis was surely dreaming . . .) Life in the basement at Danko's house was so casual that by the time, years later, it was decided to release cleaned-up versions of the songs to counter the multitude of bootleg recordings, the boys found they hadn't taken pictures (besides those of the Band themselves, outside the house). So they scuttled together a sort of down-home, basement variety *Sgt. Pepper's* cover shoot.

Nashville Skyline, however, released in 1969, was not nearly as good and was even more "country," with Dylan suddenly affecting a faux twang in his singing. It spun off the hit "Lay, Lady, Lay" and included that fascinating duet with Johnny Cash on "Girl from the North Country," with the flat-as-a-pancake but still engaging "truuue love of miiyyiiine" at the end, but the entire record had Dylan diehards scratching their heads. Was he heading into a decline, his first slump since he started recording? If Dylan knew that the question

was in the air (and surely he did), then he should never have issued *Self Portrait* in 1970, his second double-disc album but not even in the arena with *Blonde on Blonde* in terms of achievement. There were bad cover versions (how dare he do this to "Early Morning Rain" and "Let It Be Me"?), tossed-off renderings of traditional tunes, a few uninspired originals, a couple of live versions of previous hits, a general malaise. The *Rolling Stone* review by Greil Marcus put the matter succinctly in its first sentence: "What is this [expletive]?"

Dylan later hemmed and hawed, at different times claiming that the album was a joke, or that he had still been recovering from the motorcycle accident, or that he was fighting bootleggers by putting out his own bootleg. But facts were facts, and for the first time in Dylan's life, he was recording and releasing bad tracks, and he wasn't writing more than an occasional tune that was worth a lick. When *New Morning* came out only four months after *Self Portrait*—rushed to press, perhaps, to stem the tide?—it was hailed as a comeback, but in retrospect it wasn't a patch on *Highway 61*, just multifold better than *Self Portrait*.

He did have one semi-triumph in this period: his 1969 appearance at the Isle of Wight Festival in England. Another

- -

Much of the photography of Dylan in Woodstock, including all of it on these two pages, was taken by Elliott Landy, who was the one person to whom Bob granted access in this interesting, personal period. The Dylan visual record is all the richer for this allowance. Opposite: Landy remembers Bob exclaiming, "Take one like this!" on a fun day at the Ohayo Mountain Road house. In the sequence, from top, Bob is on the trampoline with Jesse, Anna and Maria; then holding Anna; then flying on his own. Below: with Anna again. Happy days of Little League games and cookouts and bouncing in the backyard with the kids . . .

big rock fest had come to his doorstep, and that is perhaps why the ever-contrary Dylan chose not to perform at Woodstock. He was put off by disciples constantly making their Dylan pilgrimage, to the point where he bought a townhouse back in the Village, on MacDougal Street, and briefly moved his family into the city. But the fans found him there, too, and he was becoming frustrated by his inability to find true peace and solace. Perhaps choosing the Isle of Wight Festival over Woodstock was some kind of message: *I'm outta here.*

Since he had not performed live, except for brief appearances at benefit concerts, in three years, this became a very big deal. Dylan was billed over the Who and Free, and it was clear that the concert, at the very end of August, would draw tens of thousands—in the event, 150,000. Of course, Dylan's backing musicians would be his recent cohorts, the Band, and he and the group ensconced themselves at Foreland Farm in Bembridge to rehearse. They were joined there briefly by John Lennon and Ringo Starr (George Harrison and his wife, Pattie Boyd, were already staying as Bob and Sara's house guests): royalty showing support to royalty. (And these Beatles would be at the concert, as would Keith Richards and Bill Wyman of the Rolling Stones, Eric Clapton, Elton John and, just by the way, Jane Fonda.) Dylan's performance was fine and went over well enough; nothing earth-shaking, but considering the circumstances and what was at stake, a solid win. He and his friends partied happily afterwards.

He's about to re-enter the game. On August 28, 1969, Dylan relaxes by the sea in England before his planned headline appearance at the Isle of Wight Festival, beginning two days hence. We invite you to play "Where's Waldo?" with the picture below: In the concert audience are John Lennon and Yoko Ono, George and Pattie Harrison, Ringo and Maureen Starkey; one point for each Beatle, two for each spouse. Opposite: On the "Day of the Locusts," June 9, 1970, in spite of the fact that (as he says in the song) "there was little to say, there was no conversation," Dylan chats with Coretta Scott King after each receives an honorary degree at Princeton University in New Jersey. He's becoming *august*.

And now what?

The phrase *Dylan didn't know what to do next* is invalid because often through the years Dylan didn't seem to know what to do, or care about what he was about to do—he just did whatever he did, next. In 1971 he allowed *Tarantula* to be published, for goodness' sake. (Well, it had a compelling cover photo.) And that year, he made his first public appearance since the Isle of Wight, taking the stage at Madison Square Garden in New York City for his friend George Harrison's benefit concerts for Bangladesh relief. He also recorded "Watching the River Flow," which is about time passing by, and "George Jackson," which is about a Black Panther who recently had been killed in San Quentin Prison. So he was either chillin', or returning to the political fray. Or maybe he was looking for something

altogether new: In late 1972 and early '73, Dylan acted in Sam Peckinpah's western *Pat Garrett and Billy the Kid*, playing the role of Alias, one of Billy's cohorts. He contributed the ethereal "Knockin' on Heaven's Door" to the soundtrack. He was all over the place, and he was nowhere in particular.

What he wasn't doing is what had made him famous: producing landmark albums and playing (regularly) to the people. Would he ever do these things again? The betting, in the early '70s, was that he would not. The betting was that he could not—not anymore.

It is interesting to consider what Dylan's legacy might have been without his second act. Had he simply diminished and then vanished after the motorcycle accident, he might have forever been one of those "'60s Icons"—in his case, the frizzy-haired folksinger who also made "Like a Rolling Stone." That's a pretty good legacy, surely, but it would not have been enough for Dylan. He was far from done.

In 1973 he recorded *Planet Waves* with the Band, and on that album was "Forever Young." Said Dylan, "I wrote it thinking about one of my boys and not wanting to be too sentimental." Jakob Dylan, Bob and Sara's youngest child, has always felt the song is for him. It probably was—but also for Bob himself, who was now only in his earliest 30s, but had somehow lived a long time. Adult problems were surfacing, and he and Sara were about to head into the dissolution of their marriage.

What caused it?

As with many broken bonds, it is difficult to definitively say. There were certainly mitigating factors. "Marriage was a failure," Dylan later said. "Husband and wife was a failure, but father and mother wasn't a failure. I wasn't a very good husband . . . I don't know what a good husband is. I was good

in some ways . . . and not so good in other ways."

So: mitigating factors. We could investigate this pruriently, but with Dylan there is no profit in it. What is interesting is a look at a man who was 73 years old when he came into Dylan's life, a man named Norman Raeben.

In 1974 some of Sara's friends came to visit, and Dylan remembered later, "They were talking about truth and love and beauty and all these words I had heard for years, and they had 'em all defined. I couldn't believe it . . . I asked them, 'Where do you come up with all those definitions?' And they told me about this teacher." The teacher was in New York City, and what he taught—what he literally taught—was painting. In the spring of 1974, Dylan visited: "He says, 'You wanna paint?' So I said, 'Well, I was thinking about it, you know.' He said, 'Well, I don't know if you even deserve to be here. Let me see what you can do.'"

It is somewhere between complicated and impossible to explain how Raeben, having agreed to take Dylan on as a pupil, influenced the singer thereafter. Dylan, a guru to many, has always been willing to accept gurus—Woody Guthrie, Dave Van Ronk (it can be said), and now Norman Raeben. For two months Dylan went to Raeben's eleventh-floor studio in Carnegie Hall and took lessons five days a week, and then "I'd just think about it the other two days of the week."

"He talked all the time," Dylan remembered, "from eight-thirty to four, and he talked in seven languages. He would tell me about myself when I was doing something, drawing something. I couldn't paint. I thought I could. I couldn't draw. I don't even remember 90 percent of the stuff he drove into me . . . I had met magicians, but this guy is more powerful than any magician I've ever met. He looked into you and told

HENRY DILTZ/CORBIS

BARRY FEINSTEIN

WARING ABBOTT/MICHAEL OCHS/GETTY

Opposite: In 1974, even covered up against the cold in Chicago, Dylan remains nevertheless distinctly recognizable. He is more plainly his famous self when he is actively giving back, as he has done before and will again. At left, he is with his dear friend George Harrison at George's Concert for Bangladesh in New York City. Below, he is with dear friends Arlo Guthrie and Dave Van Ronk in the same town for the 1974 Friends of Chile concert. Van Ronk and Harrison have since passed away; Guthrie and Dylan are still singing.

you what you were. And he didn't play games about it. If you were interested in coming out of that, you could stay there and force yourself to come out of it. You yourself did all the work. He was just some kind of guide, or something like that."

In Norman Raeben, Dylan had encountered an art teacher who was a psychoanalyst and mystic to boot, and he bought into Raeben fully. Always an inward-looking person, Dylan began to look even more deeply into his soul, and there were consequences, for suddenly Sara seemed strange to him, and he seemed strange to Sara. "It changed me," he said. "I went home after that and my wife never did understand me since that day. That's when our marriage started breaking up. She never knew what I was talking about, what I was thinking about. And I couldn't possibly explain it." The acrimonious split would not be finalized in formal divorce until 1977, when Sara would receive a large settlement of perhaps as much as $10 million, primary custody of the children, and temporary rights to live in the house in Malibu.

Norman Raeben often goes missing in the major Dylan biographies, and this is curious since Dylan did talk about him—something he doesn't do when he wants a thing to go missing. Perhaps it is that the Raeben episode and influence seem simply too weird for Dylanophiles (and writers), who have weirdness a-plenty to deal with already. The last thing they require is a septuagenarian Yoda guiding

Bobby through a pre-midlife crisis.

But facts are facts, and Dylan himself didn't shy from them. He saw Raeben as an instrument in the dissolution of his marriage—a thing that pained him deeply, as "[I] figured it would last forever . . . I believe in marriage"—and also in his renaissance as a songwriter and musician. In an interview with *Rolling Stone*'s Jonathan Cott after the motorcycle accident, he confessed to his problems with songwriting: "Since that point, I more or less had amnesia. Now you can take that statement as literally or as metaphysically as you need to, but that's what happened to me. It took me a long time to get to do consciously what I used to do unconsciously." He said of his attempts to write for *Nashville Skyline*, "[I]t didn't go nowhere—it just went down, down, down . . . I was convinced I wasn't going to do anything else."

And then he had the "good fortune" to encounter Raeben, "who taught me how to see . . . He put my mind and my hand and my eye together, in a way that allowed me to do consciously what I unconsciously felt."

Separated from Sara and his family but pining for them, examining what had gone wrong, Dylan began to write the songs that would fill his paramount album, *Blood on the Tracks*. He focused on the concept of "no time": "You've got yesterday, today and tomorrow all in the same room, and there's very little that you can't imagine happening." Raeben was a spirit on his shoulder: "I was just trying to make it like a painting where you can see the different parts but then you also see the whole of it . . . with the concept of time, and the way the characters change from the first person to the third person, and you're never quite sure if the third person is talking or the first person is talking. But as you look at the whole thing, it really doesn't matter."

True enough.

Whether it was the first or third person, and whatever road or sage had delivered him to this point, Dylan was talking again. Speaking to us.

In words and music well worth listening to.

Dylan always loved art and painting, and became ever more serious about it after his tutoring by Norman Raeben. Here he is in 1974 at the Phillips Collection in Washington, D.C., where he appreciates the French artist Pierre Bonnard's 1918 canvas "The Terrace." In the background, bearded, is his friend Louis Kemp. Kemp was from back in Minnesota; Dylan stuck through the years with several of the guys Bobby Zimmerman had known. Kemp was sometimes on the road with Dylan—he helped manage the Rolling Thunder Revue tour, which we will learn about beginning four pages on—and also ran Kemp Fisheries in Duluth ("smoked salmon to The Last Waltz"). It is clear from reading _Chronicles: Volume One_ that Dylan, in his seniority, has become his better self, probably his best self. He has no more hills to climb, during which effort he might once have climbed over others, or positioned himself so that others might pull him up. He can't release music without everybody buying it. He can't show up without everyone wanting to watch and listen. Everything he might have been desperate for is now guaranteed, and he can just relax—and ask his boyhood friends what they think of the painting.

Dylan at the Movies

Did you know he won an Academy Award? He won his Oscar for writing the 2001 song from *The Wonder Boys*, "Things Have Changed." He appeared himself in fascinating documentaries, feature films ranging from westerns to near auto-biographies, and also the never-to-be-categorized *Renaldo and Clara*. And he has been memorably portrayed by others, including one of the world's finest actresses.

RENALDO & CLARA

NOW SHOWING!   NOW SHOWING!

Starring

BOB DYLAN & JOAN BAEZ

Written and Directed by Bob Dylan   Produced by Lombard Street Films, Inc.
Distributed Worldwide by Circuit Films   Metrocolor   R. RESTRICTED

THE PLAYERS

Renaldo	**BOB DYLAN**
Clara	**SARA DYLAN**
The Woman In White	**JOAN BAEZ**
Bob Dylan	**RONNIE HAWKINS**
Mrs. Dylan	**RONEE BLAKLEY**
Longhena de Castro	**JACK ELLIOTT**
Lafkezio	**HARRY DEAN STANTON**
The Masked Tortilla	**BOB NEUWIRTH**
The Father	**ALLEN GINSBERG**
Mandolin Player	**ARLO GUTHRIE**
Guest Artist	**ROBERTA FLACK**
Musicians	**ROLLING THUNDER REVIEW**

Exclusive Engagement

Galeria Cinema
57 Boylston St.
Harvard Sq.
661-3737
SHOWN AT 1:30 & 7:30

BARRY FEINSTEIN

ANDREW WALKER/GETTY

WEINSTEIN COMPANY/EVERETT

Opposite, clockwise from top left: Dylan is filmed by documentarian D.A. Pennebaker for 1967's *Dont Look Back;* he plays Alias in Sam Peckinpah's 1973 *Pat Garrett and Billy the Kid;* a poster for his own auteur turn in 1978; he takes his cue in 1987's *Hearts of Fire.* Above: The photograph Martin Scorsese chose to represent his 2005 documentary *No Direction Home.* Far left: A musical based on Dylan's music bombs on Broadway in 2006. Left: Cate Blanchett portrays a Dylan-like character and David Cross renders Allen Ginsberg in the 2007 film *I'm Not There.*

Rolling On

W̲ho was Rolling Thunder? Even deep-dyed Dylanologists might be interested to know that he was a real person: a modern-day Cherokee shaman who, through marriage to Spotted Fawn, joined the Shoshone of Nevada. He was a medicine man, a teacher and, eventually, a symbol. Also called John Pope in the non-Indian world, he became an activist not just for Native American rights but for environmental causes and equality for women. In 1975 he and Spotted Fawn founded Meta Tantay ("Go in Peace"), a 262-acre intertribal, interracial community—a super commune that would last for about a decade. He was, in the meantime and even earlier, noticed by others out West, and was involved in three Billy Jack films as well as on *Rolling Thunder*, an album by the Grateful Dead drummer Mickey Hart. So this was the Rolling Thunder for which Bob Dylan's famous concert tour of 1975 and '76 was named.

But wait!

We're dealing with Dylan here, so . . . Maybe not.

It has been said by others that the tour was named for Operation Rolling Thunder, a U.S. aerial bombardment campaign conducted during the Vietnam War.

But would Dylan really do that? Name a loose-limbed, organo-groovy musical tour after a military exercise?

Well, he was Dylan, and you never know . . .

The man himself said, in one of those altogether-too-easy explanations, "I was just sitting outside my house one day thinking about a name for this tour, when all of a sudden, I looked into the sky and I heard a boom! Then, boom, boom, boom, boom, rolling from west to east. So I figured that should be the name."

Yeah, sure.

Right, Bobby. And the song "Sara" wasn't about Sara.

Whatever you say.

For our part, we're still taken with the Native American story. We figure someone must have mentioned Rolling Thunder and Spotted Fawn to Dylan—and besides, Rolling Thunder himself hung with the tour for a few dates. The Native American story seems a much neater fit considering the spirit that would imbue the tour. And when piecing together Dylan, it's usually a good idea to take the best available fit.

He does it himself, all the time.

In 1975, restless to hit the road, Dylan wanted a soulful, old-timey, medicine show–type tour of the Northeast, and he got it in spades, starting out in Plymouth, Massachusetts, where once the Pilgrims had struggled to weather the winter.

Safe to say, few in New England knew much about John Pope/Rolling Thunder in '75. And few knew of Bob Dylan's latest move, which was heading their way.

Pulitzer Prize–winning playwright Sam Shepard's impressionistic *Rolling Thunder Logbook* remains the best (and certainly the most fun) delineation of those crazy days and that crazy tour.

Some brief preface material to Shepard's remembrances: Bobby and Sara were on the rocks, they were fighting over custody of the kids, he was itching to get out on the road again. The Rolling Thunder Revue, under whatever name, had been boiling in his head for years, and it started to seem like the next idea to act upon.

There was a message on a green piece of notepaper waiting for Shepard at his California ranch: "Dylan called." It had a return number.

Shepard was thoroughly mystified. He didn't know Dylan, any Dylan, certainly not *the* Dylan. He returned the call, and:

"I get an entangled series of secretaries, lawyers, business managers, each one with a guarded approach.

"'Shepard? Shepard who? Are you the one who killed his wife?'

"'No, I'm the astronaut.'

"'Oh. Well, what's this all about? Why did Dylan call you?'

"'That's what I'm calling you about.'

"'Oh. Well, just a minute. I'll see if I can find somebody.'

"The phone goes blank and then a new voice. A man voice.

Then blank again. Then a woman voice. Then back to a man.

"'Yes, Mr. Shepard. Let me explain. Bob is going on a secret tour in the Northeast. He's calling it Rolling Thunder—the Rolling Thunder Revue.'

"There's something about the way this chump is calling Dylan 'Bob' that immediately pisses me off, combined with the confusion of trying to figure out where in the hell the Northeast is exactly. Before I know it, something hostile is coming out of my mouth.

"'If it's so secret, how come you're telling me about it?'"

Dylan was telling Shepard about it because he wanted him in New York City within a day or two to begin work on a film of this weird tour he had planned. The singer envisioned a kind of neorealistic docu-comedy, something influenced by the French nouvelle vague, if we can judge by his byplay with Shepard, as remembered by Shepard:

"'Did you ever see *Children of Paradise*?' he says. I admit I have but a long time ago. I saw it with a girl who cried all the way through so it's hard to relate my exact impressions. 'How about *Shoot the Piano Player*?'

"'Yeah, I saw that one too. Is that the kind of movie you want to make?'

"'Something like that.'"

The Shepard project never came to pass, although there was a lot of film shot during the tour—concert footage as well as improvised scenes starring Dylan and his friends. This would all wind up in *Renaldo and Clara*, a nearly five-hour movie for which Shepard can scarcely be blamed. Nonetheless, even as his role as screenwriter was quietly dissolving because musicians who were performing each evening would hardly be memorizing dialogue at breakfast, Shepard continued to hang out, and thereby piled up the reminiscences and observations contained in his logbook. We are all the richer for this.

What was the Rolling Thunder Revue all about? The quick answer is, "Hard to say . . . this and that . . ."—but that's a cop-out. It was, in fact, one of Dylan's smartest notions. It was a fun, friendly get-together with his musical friends and most devoted fans, a barnstorming musical caravan and nightly revival meeting. It was, in a way that some of his earlier and later concerts were not, extremely generous. It was a marvelous and surprising re-entry into the day-to-day of show business. The music was uniformly wonderful. The spirit was, too.

In terms of DNA, the Rolling Thunder Revue was something of a cross between an old-time medicine show, Ed Sullivan's Sunday night TV program and Garrison Keillor's

Left: Dylan with Allen Ginsberg, Rolling Thunder's resident poet. Below: Meeting with the ex-boxer Rubin "Hurricane" Carter, who had been convicted in a triple-murder and became one of the tour's chief causes when Dylan sang his new protest song, "Hurricane," night after night. (Carter was eventually freed, and went on to become an advocate for the wrongfully accused.) Opposite: Dylan listening to a recording during a break in a Rolling Thunder rehearsal.

A Prairie Home Companion. There wasn't a comedian or juggler or Topo Gigio, but there was a poet (Allen Ginsberg), who served much the same purpose. In the large and jangly band there was David Bowie's "Spiders from Mars" guitarist, Mick Ronson, and from Dylan's very earliest days in the Village, Ramblin' Jack Elliott. There was Joan Baez for the first time in 10 years, and Roger McGuinn of the Byrds. There was the exotic violinist Scarlet Rivera, whom Dylan had recruited after seeing her walking down the street, her violin case slung over her back, and there was also Ronee Blakley, a fine country singer who had just made her acting debut in Robert Altman's *Nashville.* As the tour gained steam, there were guest stars: Joni Mitchell, Bruce Springsteen, Patti Smith and others who wanted in on this wacky, hey-kids-let's-put-on-a-show idea. Taken in all—both in the more spontaneous regional 1975 leg of the tour and the 1976 second act that moved into larger halls in bigger cities nationwide—perhaps one hundred performers took the stage with the revue at one point or another. Even, as said, the real Rolling Thunder himself: "[He] showed up all the way from the West and performed a special Tobacco Ceremony at the break of dawn, with all the main stars involved," wrote Shepard.

The true magic was in the first concerts, in Plymouth and North Dartmouth and Lowell and Springfield, Massachusetts; in Providence, Rhode Island; Durham, New Hampshire;

Burlington, Vermont. At the very first of these, the potential audience still wasn't quite sure whether to believe the rumors: that this was a Dylan tour. The fans had *heard* that it *might* be him, but he had been out of the spotlight for so long, these hopefuls had to buy tickets on faith alone. There was no guarantee.

And then, there he was, often in whiteface makeup, almost always in the flat-brimmed gaucho hat, singing as well and as passionately as he ever had. (The music from the first concerts was finally released in 2002 on the album *Live 1975: The Rolling Thunder Revue.*) Dylan was back, no doubt about that. He was back, and at his very best.

The versions of old songs—he and Baez opening the second half of the show from behind the curtain, their vocals on "Blowin' in the Wind" coming out of nowhere—were mesmeric, and the renderings of new ones—the songs from *Blood on the Tracks* and now *Desire*, particularly an incendiary take on "Isis"—were startling. Dylan traveled auditorium to auditorium, all these ideas swimming in his head: What should we shoot for the movie? What do we add to this night's show? What's the deal with me and Joan? Me and Sara? Me and . . .

Shepard observes it all, and most of his note-taking is semi-journalistic and in service to a sort of narrative. But occasionally he just muses, and there is this: "Dylan has invented himself. He's made himself up from scratch. That is, from the

If the Golden Chords of Hibbing, Minnesota, had become marginally (well, a bit above marginally) more successful, they might have enjoyed a town-to-town tour like Rolling Thunder's early days. That seemed to be what Dylan was imagining. Opposite, clockwise from top: He and Baez rehearse backstage in a bare-bones setting; he and Ginsberg visit Jack Kerouac's grave during an early stopover in Lowell, Massachusetts; the two former lovers reminisce about their earlier romance, in Becket, Massachusetts. Left: No dressing rooms, but locker rooms. It's fun to remember, when looking at the two lower pictures on this page, that Dylan rehearsed his rock band in a Newport mansion the night before he "went electric" in 1965. Precisely a decade later, he and his "merry players" romp on the beach below the Breakers, the very grandest pile of marble in that grand Rhode Island town, a mansion built by Cornelius Vanderbilt. In the photo at bottom—another scene being filmed for possible inclusion in the imagined future film—Dylan tootles on the trumpet and T-Bone Burnett plays guitar, serenading diners Ronee Blakley and Bob Neuwirth.

----

things he had around him and inside him. Dylan is an invention of his own mind. The point isn't to figure him out but to take him in. He gets into you anyway, so why not just take him in? He's not the first one to have invented himself, but he's the first one to have invented Dylan. No one invented him before him. Or after."

Any fans who did place a bet and did see the Rolling Thunder Revue in the early days came away thinking two things: That's as close to Dylan—the great Dylan—as I'll ever get. And: Lucky me.

The fans who went to the last-ever appearances of the Rolling Thunder Revue in the spring of '76 probably had a different take. As the show moved through the Orlando Sports Stadium and University of Florida Field in Gainesville in late April, the initial thrill was gone, the gas draining by dribs and drabs. "The Rolling Thunder Revue, so joyful and electrifying in its first performances, had just plain run out of steam," wrote Janet Maslin in *Rolling Stone*. Indeed, something that had been built on imagination and spontaneity suffered in its middle age, when those impetuses had since evaporated. Dylan wanted to preserve what had occurred, of course—all that filming, after all—and in late May he scheduled a couple of final dates, and arranged for a Colorado concert to be filmed and recorded for the *Hard Rain* NBC TV special and companion live album. Only a few days later, the Rolling Thunder Revue, unquestionably one of the greatest-ever rock tours, played to a half-empty capacity-17,000 Salt Palace in Salt Lake City.

Perhaps Dylan, too, was dispirited by the denouement. Or maybe the breakup of his marriage was not a thing that Rolling Thunder had proved any kind of antidote for. But anyway: He would do the occasional one-off appearance, but

wouldn't tour or record new material for yet another two years. His hiatus from public life, brilliantly and rapturously interrupted by the Rolling Thunder Revue, was back in force.

Except for a memorable performance at one very special gig.

Dylan went away in 1976 with his canisters containing 240,000 feet (100 hours!) of film and started stitching together *Renaldo and Clara*—meanwhile wondering if he could stitch together his marriage, which would not prove possible—as the acclaimed movie director Martin Scorsese was embarking on quite another project that would result in a more enduring film. Scorsese had gotten to know the Band's Robbie Robertson, with whom he would collaborate on film music for years, and he knew of that group's intention to end its career as a touring act (even though other members of the Band were displeased with Robertson's plans to quit the road). Robertson wanted to film a farewell concert, and once Scorsese got involved the affair grew into a production involving a 300-page shooting script, scads of camera operators,

5,000 fortunate attendees at San Francisco's Winterland Ballroom, dinner and dancing before the show, and then a concert, beginning at 9 p.m., that included not only the Band but Eric Clapton, Emmylou Harris, Joni Mitchell, Van Morrison, Ringo Starr, Muddy Waters, Neil Young, bizarrely Neil Diamond, a half dozen other performers and, of course, Ronnie Hawkins (who had years ago fronted the Hawks, and who was one of the "stars" of the *Renaldo and Clara* footage) and Bob Dylan. Cocaine was as generously ladled that night as gravy for the Thanksgiving turkey supper, and there were rough and ragged moments to be sure, but *The Last Waltz*— film and soundtrack—lives on as an essential rock 'n' roll document. And, as Terry Curtis Fox would write in the *Village Voice*, "While ostensibly . . . about the Band, Scorsese's editing makes no bones about how much a Dylan event it became . . . Everything else disappears behind his presence. Scorsese . . . does nothing to hide or minimalize this effect."

Interestingly, it was by no means certain, until the last moment, that Dylan would take the stage. He was there at

At left, Bill Graham is onstage with Dylan before a show. The year is 1975, and Graham, America's preeminent rock concert promoter, is soon to take on the intricate planning of The Last Waltz, the swan song performance of a group with which he has long been affiliated: the Band. That show, which will live on forever in Martin Scorsese's film, will take place in San Francisco, Graham's home base, and will of course feature Bob Dylan (below, with his Band mates Rick Danko, Robbie Robertson and Garth Hudson on the night of the Waltz).

Winterland, for sure, but was balking at being filmed, concerned that Scorsese's movie would steal thunder from *Renaldo and Clara* if it was released first. In the end, he did perform, and Scorsese later remembered the promoter Bill Graham at his shoulder shouting, "'Shoot him! Shoot him! He comes from the same streets as you. Don't worry, don't let him push you around.' Nevertheless, we got our cues right and we shot the two songs that were used in the film." And those songs, for history's sake, were "Baby, Let Me Follow You Down" and "Forever Young."

After the Band's early morning encore of "Don't Do It" on November 26, 1976, the classic lineup of that well-traveled rock 'n' roll ensemble essentially retired: It would never perform together onstage again. Dylan went back into hiding, and back to work on his movie. *Renaldo and Clara* was released in 1978. The *Village Voice*, which had once lionized its fellow downtown citizen Dylan, dispatched no fewer than seven reviewers to deal with this remarkable 292-minute thing. "Did you see the firing squad of critics they sent?"

an obviously wounded Dylan asked Robert Shelton. Wrote James Walcott in one of the broadsides, claiming the film was sinking a whole bunch of theretofore estimable reputations: "It's like watching the defeat of the Spanish Armada." More insightful was Pauline Kael in *The New Yorker*: "Despite all his masks and camouflage [he's] still the same surly, mystic tease . . . more tight close-ups than any actor can have had in the whole history of movies. He's overpoweringly present, yet he is never in direct contact with us . . . we are invited to stare . . . to perceive the mystery of his elusiveness—his distance."

Indeed. A central paradox of Dylan's life and career is that he has always encouraged—actively courted—the staring, and then, as he rails on about it for pages in *Chronicles: Volume One*, has not only recoiled from the effects of it but blamed the staring on others, as if he had nothing to do with it. Certainly when disciples were knocking on his door in Woodstock or protesting outside his New York City apartment building that he needed to return to the political fray, that was much too much. It was bad, even threatening behavior. But just as certainly, when Dylan writes, "No place was far enough away. I don't know what everybody else was fantasizing about but what I was fantasizing about was a nine-to-five existence, a house on a tree-lined block with a white picket fence, pink roses in the backyard. That would have been nice. That was my deepest dream"—well, when he writes that, and then issues *Renaldo and Clara* and then returns to the road later in 1978 for a world tour that eventually encompasses 114 shows and plays to 2 million people grossing $20 million, the only reaction can possibly be: *Really?*

If so, Bob, you truly *were* dreaming.

The album *Street Legal*, recorded in April of 1978 in California (where Dylan was then living, and continues to live today, with places in Minnesota and New York as well) completed what can be argued as another landmark triptych: *Blood on the Tracks, Desire* and *Street Legal.* These were intensely personal, inward-looking records brimful with some of the most emotionally moving songs he ever wrote, even if Dylan subsequently disclaimed that they had anything to do with his own life: Chekhov, ancient mythology, the weather, whatever all else—they had absolutely nothing to do with him, *nothing.* Dylan's fans weren't eager to argue the matter.

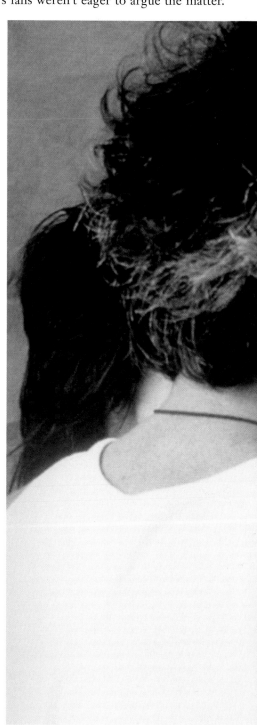

Although the Never-Ending Tour will start in 1988, Dylan was ready to get back out there in 1984—and he did so, in support of his album *Infidels.* While in Ireland during that road show, he told war stories for the folks at the trailer used by the reggae/pop band UB40 (above) and was happy to pose with Bono of the rock band U2 and MTV's Martha Quinn (left). Right: The following year, Dylan is backed at the Live Aid concert by Rolling Stones guitarist Keith Richards, who is pictured here in a huddle with movie star Jack Nicholson. No need to indicate "left to right" with these three, yes?

Having him back onstage and producing great record after great record, the fans in the stands were delighted. Their favorite pitcher was throwing fastballs again.

But right about now, how about a not atypical curveball from Bobby Zimmerman?

How about Jesus?

In the early months of 1979, Dylan took Bible study classes at the Vineyard School of Discipleship in Reseda, California, and its pastor later recalled that two of the school's associates eventually "went over to Bob's house and ministered to him. He responded by saying, Yes, he did in fact want Christ in his life. And he prayed that day and received the Lord."

As happens with many converts, he threw himself into this new pursuit, even unto trying to evangelize producer Jerry Wexler while making his next record, *Slow Train Coming*, an overture that Wexler politely deflected: "Bob, you're dealing with a 62-year-old confirmed Jewish atheist. I'm hopeless. Let's make an album." They made a wonderful one, full of modern gospel music, including the Dylan classic "Gotta Serve Somebody." The follow-up collection, *Saved*, was not nearly as good, and the concerts given in this period were, to many Dylan fans, more mystifying than revelatory. Their

reticent sage who used to say absolutely nothing—not a word—between songs was now preaching to them at considerable (some felt insufferable) length: "[T]hey say, 'Yes, you are a prophet.' I said, 'No, it's not me.' They used to say, 'You sure are a prophet.' They used to convince me I was a prophet. Now I come out and say Jesus Christ is the answer. They say, 'Bob Dylan's no prophet.' They just can't handle it."

If the audience wasn't shouting "Amen!" to that—and it usually wasn't—it was more upset that Dylan was refusing to sing any of their requests, most of which were for songs from his long, previous, secular period.

Dylan would return to those forsaken songs, of course, and would vacillate on religion as the years progressed. "Here's the thing with me and the religious thing," he said to David Gates of *Newsweek* in 1997. "This is the flat-out truth: I find religiosity and philosophy in the music. I don't find it anywhere else. Songs like 'Let Me Rest on a Peaceful Mountain'

or 'I Saw the Light'—that's my religion. I don't adhere to rabbis, preachers, evangelists, all of that. I've learned more from the songs than I have learned from any of this kind of entity. The songs are my entity. I believe the songs." But he always made it clear, as well, that he did believe in God—*a* god, some god. Important to note: He has spent the recent decades of his life involved in the Jewish Chabad-Lubavitch movement, appearing on telethons, and told Ed Bradley on *60 Minutes* in 2004, "the only person you have to think about lying twice to is either yourself or to God." When Bill Flanagan said in a 2009 interview that Dylan delivered "O Little Town of Bethlehem" like "a true believer" on his *Christmas in the Heart* album, Dylan replied pleasantly, "Well, I am a true believer."

On January 31, 1986, Desiree Gabrielle Dennis-Dylan was born at Humana Hospital in Canoga Park, California, with a father listed on the birth certificate as Robert

On these pages: Friends from the '80s and '90s. At left is the super-group the Traveling Wilburys featuring, from left, Otis Wilbury, also known as Clayton (also known as Jeff Lynne); Lucky, also known as Boo (and as the subject of this book); Nelson, also known as Spike (sometimes called George Harrison); and Charlie T. Wilbury Jr., also known as Muddy (and sometimes Tom Petty). Below, at his induction into the Rock and Roll Hall of Fame in 1988, Dylan harmonizes with, from left, Al Jardine, Mike Love, Mick Jagger, Bruce Springsteen and Mary Wilson.

NEAL PRESTON/CORBIS (2)

Dylan. On June 4 of that year, Carolyn Dennis, the baby's mom, and Bob Dylan wed. Their union would last six years, during which time Carolyn would continue as one of Dylan's gospel-rock backup singers, occasionally joined by her own mother, who had earlier been a member of Ray Charles's Raelettes. Also during this time, Dylan would dedicate his 1990 album, *Under the Red Sky*, to "Gabby Goo Goo," who was, he told absolutely no one, his toddler, Desiree.

Carolyn had started working for Dylan in 1978, and eventually began dating him—as had and did other African American women in his entourage. "I think he [dated] some of these black girls because they didn't idolize him," the singer Maria Muldaur told Dylan biographer Howard Sounes. "They were real down to earth, and they didn't worship him. [They are] strong women who would just say, cut off your [bull]."

Dylan was, by accounts, just as good a parent to Desiree as he had been to his children with Sara, and she was later given the choice as to whether to keep his surname as part of her own—which she decided to do. Although Dylan's now almost feral instinct to keep his private life *private* was well in play—and the wider world would not know of this second marriage until years after it had ended—Carolyn Dennis later said in his defense, "To portray Bob as hiding his daughter is just malicious and ridiculous. That is something he would never do. Bob has been a wonderful, active father to Desiree."

She continued: "Bob and I made a choice to keep our marriage a private matter for a simple reason—to give our daughter a normal childhood." The couple utilized a California law that allowed them to keep their marriage certificate sealed from public disclosure, and in 1992 Dylan used "R. Zimmerman" as his listing in the divorce settlement—another file that was ordered sealed by a judge.

Why this marriage didn't last longer probably has to do with Dylan's later-in-life (or perhaps, considering how far he

had come since Hibbing, lifelong) peripatetic nature. After Bob decided to go without backup singers altogether, Carolyn settled down at their home in Tarzana, California, while her husband embarked, in 1988, on what would eventually be called his Never-Ending Tour. He came home from time to time, but "time to time" is never enough, and Carolyn eventually called the marriage quits.

There have been unsubstantiated rumors that Dylan married other women through the years, or might have fathered other children, and these rumors can be chased effortlessly on the Internet if one chooses to do so. A life lived as clandestinely as Dylan's encourages rumors. But what we know for sure: Twice he tried to make a family; twice he succeeded; and twice he hit the road again.

This time, he hit the road in earnest—he hit the road for good, seemingly forevermore.

Since 1980 he had been singing the old songs again as well as the new, and clearly this decision, at least, made everybody happy. In the mid-1980s he had done a couple of mega tours with famous friends—Tom Petty and the Heartbreakers, the Grateful Dead—and these were well attended, but, frankly, even on the Dylan classics, they just weren't Dylan. He performed at well-intentioned benefits such as Live Aid in 1985, but the performance was uneven at best, Keith Richards's backing notwithstanding. He made a bunch of albums—*Shot of Love* (including the wonderful "Every Grain of Sand"), *Infidels*, *Empire Burlesque*, *Knocked Out Loaded* (including the greatly underappreciated 11-minute collaboration with Sam Shepard, "Brownsville Girl"), *Down in the Groove*—that did little to dispel the general notion that the great bulk of Dylan's

best music was behind him. His guest vocal on rapper Kurtis Blow's 1986 offering *Kingdom Blow* only served as a confirmer.

And then, on June 7, 1988, all of the wandering came to an end, and the renaissance began.

(Noted: Dylan himself would recoil, perhaps violently, at that last sentence and all that it implies about any kind of slump, or different direction, or comeback.)

On that night in late spring he fronted a small, terrific, tight band led by guitarist G.E. Smith of the *Saturday Night Live* house orchestra, and everything clicked. Dylan would

You become a legend, you last a long time, you get the laurels. Opposite, from top: In 1990 in Paris, where Dylan once told an audience he was just as unhappy as they were, French Minister of Culture Jack Lang names Dylan a Commandeur dans l'Ordre des Arts et des Lettres; in 1997, Dylan stands with fellow Kennedy Center honorees Lauren Bacall, Edward Villella, Jessye Norman and Charlton Heston; that same year Dylan entertains Pope John Paul II and young people from around the world who are gathering in Rome. This page: In 2001, Dylan is immense on screen at the Shrine Auditorium in L.A. as he accepts his Oscar for Best Original Song, and in 2004 he is humble as he is bestowed his honorary Doctor of Music degree during a ceremony at University of St Andrews in Scotland.

later write, in the liner notes to his folkie 1993 album, *World Gone Wrong*, "Don't be bewildered by the Never Ending Tour chatter. There was a Never Ending Tour but it ended in '91 with the departure of guitarist G.E. Smith. That one's long gone but there have been many others since then: 'The Money Never Runs Out Tour' (Fall of '91), 'Southern Sympathizer Tour' (Early '92), 'Why Do You Look at Me So Strangely Tour' (European Tour '92), 'The One Sad Cry of Pity Tour' (Australia & West Coast America Tour '92), 'Don't Let Your Deal Go Down Tour' ('93) and others, too many to mention each with their own character & design."

That Bobby, he's a riot.

Except it didn't end, no matter what the man says, because Dylan has stayed out there, with great band after great band—all of these ensembles approximately the same functional size, and featuring master players—to this very day.

And this is the life Dylan was always aiming for: to play forever to the people, just as Lead Belly had, just as Muddy Waters had, just as B.B. King was still doing. Why not? he asked *Rolling Stone* magazine in 2009: "Critics should know that there's no such thing as forever. Does anybody ever call Henry Ford a Never Ending Car Builder? Anybody ever say that Duke Ellington was on a Never Ending Bandstand Tour? These days, people are lucky to have a job. Any job. So critics might be uncomfortable with me [working so much]. Anybody with a trade can work as long as they want. A welder, a carpenter, an electrician. They don't necessarily need to retire."

He didn't retire from the recording studio, either, and to the astonishment of even his most fervent fans, he began to make masterworks again. He closed out the 1980s with *Oh Mercy*, produced by Daniel Lanois, and some years later found himself holed up during a snowstorm at his Minnesota farm, during which time he wrote a bushel of songs he thought might be right for a second Lanois collaboration. The result was *Time Out of Mind*, which won him his first solo Grammy for Album of the Year. That was followed, as mentioned earlier in these pages, by *Love and Theft*, which went to Number Five on the Billboard charts, and *Modern Times*, which went to Number One. In 2009, *Together Through Life* debuted at that lofty position, making Bob Dylan, at 67, the oldest recording artist ever to turn the trick. (He lost that title in 2011 to Tony Bennett, who was 85 when *Duets II* bowed at Number One.)

He was rolling on, and still relevant.

Meanwhile, on the side—back in 1988—he became part of the Traveling Wilburys alongside his pals George Harrison, Roy Orbison, Tom Petty and Jeff Lynne. Harrison hated celebrity as much as Dylan seemed to, and it was fun to hide behind aliases. Dylan was Lucky Wilbury on the first album, Boo Wilbury on the second and last—which was named, of course, *Volume 3*.

"**E**ventually, different anachronisms were thrust upon me," Dylan writes in *Chronicles: Volume One*'s longish section where he talks about all the erroneous assumptions and expectations as well as the fearsome pressures that attended his fame. "Legend, Icon, Enigma (Buddha in

European Clothes was my favorite)—stuff like that, but that was all right. These titles were placid and harmless, thread-bare, easy to get around with them. Prophet, Messiah, Savior—those are tough ones."

So in his seniority, he must be okay with the "anachronisms" and accolades that have come his way, for he has never been given a Lifetime Prophet or Savior Award. If he has often been referred to as an Eternal Enigma, most of these trophies explicitly or implicitly imply Legend. Or Icon. He can get around with those.

Why do we know for sure that he has been more than okay with these many tributes that finally acknowledge the immensity of his contribution to American music and culture? Because he has shown up to accept them. He is polite now—he has grown up; the days of that drunken rant at the Tom Paine belong to a different, bygone man—and he is appreciative.

The laurels come in formal and informal form. Since the 1960s, there has been a constant stream of "new Dylans," and in a certain way this is an accolade. Some of these performers have possessed tremendous, individualistic talent—John Prine was once a new Dylan, and so was Bruce Springsteen—while others were never heard from after gaining the appellation. The intrinsically impossible search for a new Dylan, when we have the authentic (if self-invented) Dylan quite in our midst, has grown to be such a cottage industry that at one point a group called itself, perhaps hoping for attention, the New Dylans. It didn't work. Finally comes Sara and Bobby's youngest child, Jakob Dylan—literally, a new Dylan—and he is the goods, without ever having to say so.

Bob Dylan's name and story and words have become

After a long journey, Bobby Zimmerman of Hibbing, Minnesota, who is now acclaimed by just about all, is as comfortable in the halls of power as he is in his own skin. On this page, he is seen on February 9, 2010, performing in the East Room of the White House during "A Celebration of Music from the Civil Rights Movement," and then greeting the President and First Lady. Opposite: A last picture for this "Rolling On" chapter: Dylan and Allen Ginsberg, walking away, during their last tour together. The poet, certainly one of the reasons Dylan traveled as he did, died in 1997. He, Kerouac, Suze, Van Ronk, Albert Grossman, Richard Manuel, Rick Danko, George Harrison, Roy Orbison, Johnny Cash—they all have passed. Dylan—Bobby Zimmerman—carries the flame.

American touchstones. According to a 2007 study by a University of Tennessee law professor, Alex Long, the songwriter's lyrics far outdistance any of his rivals' in number of citations in legal briefs, court opinions and rulings—including by the U.S. Supreme Court: 186 instances (at that juncture in '07), with "You don't need a weatherman to know which way the wind blows," "The times they are a-changin'" and "When you ain't got nothing, you got nothing to lose" dusting the quote-worthiness of the Beatles or the Stones (the latter of whose standing at number six on the list rests largely on "You can't always get what you want," a gem of legalese if ever there was one). Dylan, in this instance, crosses all political lines, as even conservative Chief Justice John Roberts and his ultraconservative colleague Antonin Scalia have been, shall we say, guilty of citing the wisdom of Bob Dylan in their written opinions.

He has been paid tribute in realms other than music. While a gazillion cover versions of his songs have been made, and another gazillion songs directly or indirectly referencing him have been written, there is more. He has contributed himself; he has gotten the literary critics involved. *Chronicles: Volume One* almost crept up on people. They had figured that if Dylan ever finished a memoir, as it was rumored he was trying to do, it would be goofy, evasive or cryptic in the extreme. And then came this: a finely written, thoroughly engaging reminiscence with a good deal of insight and just enough candor to satisfy any reader. *Rolling Stone, The Onion* and *The Village Voice* named it a best book of 2004, but so did *The New York Times, The Economist* and *The Guardian* of London, and it was a finalist for the National Book Award. Its sequel (or sequels) will probably win Dylan his future Pulitzers.

We have already dealt, on pages 78 and 79, with Dylan the actor's contributions to film. But what about having a whole movie made about you by a hotshot director with the world's biggest stars, and you have nothing to do with it? Now *that's* a tribute. It was called *I'm Not There*, was released in 2007, was directed by Todd Haynes and starred, among several, Cate Blanchett, Christian Bale, Richard Gere and Heath Ledger as aspects of Bob Dylan, and Dylan's old friend Kris Kristofferson as the narrator. Kris and Bob used to pass the guitar in a circle at Johnny Cash's house, each of them trying out his new stuff for the other. Everything was coming around.

Those elliptical acknowledgments probably meant more to Dylan than the hardware he received, but if entertainers had a batting average in the "official awards" category, Dylan would beat Ted Williams. Of 12 Grammy nominations, he has won 10; with his one Oscar nomination for Best Original Song, he prevailed; the same song won a Golden Globe. In 1988 he was inducted into the Rock and Roll Hall of Fame ("Dylan was—he was revolutionary, man. The way Elvis freed your body, Bob freed your mind," Bruce Springsteen said in presenting him. "And he showed us that just because the music was innately physical, it did not mean that it was anti-intellect."), and in 1991 he received a Grammy Lifetime Achievement Award, this one handed over by Jack Nicholson. In 1990, France named him a Commandeur dans l'Ordre des Arts et des Lettres (which elevated him nearly to the level of Jerry Lewis). In 1997 he was a Kennedy Center honoree and a recipient of the Dorothy and Lillian Gish Prize, but even more: He performed before Pope John Paul II and 200,000 others at the 23rd Italian National Eucharistic Congress in Bologna, Italy, and listened as the Pope delivered a homily parsing "Blowin' in the Wind." In 2000 he won the Polar Music Prize, in 2002 he was inducted into the Nashville Songwriters Hall of Fame, in 2004 the University of St Andrews in Scotland gave him an honorary doctorate to add to his collection, in 2007 he won the Prince of Asturias Award for the Arts, in 2008 he was given his Pulitzer Prize Special Citation, and in 2009 he was a National Medal of Arts and National Humanities Medal honoree. He had, in a way of speaking, cleared the table.

His albums were shooting right to the top, he was playing to the people night after night, he had the acclaim of all and the love of many.

Was that the way he had imagined it when he told his mom and dad that he was going to hitchhike to New York City and give it a try, and they had said: Okay, we'll give you a year?

Bob Dylan, after all.

Maybe so.

Maybe so.

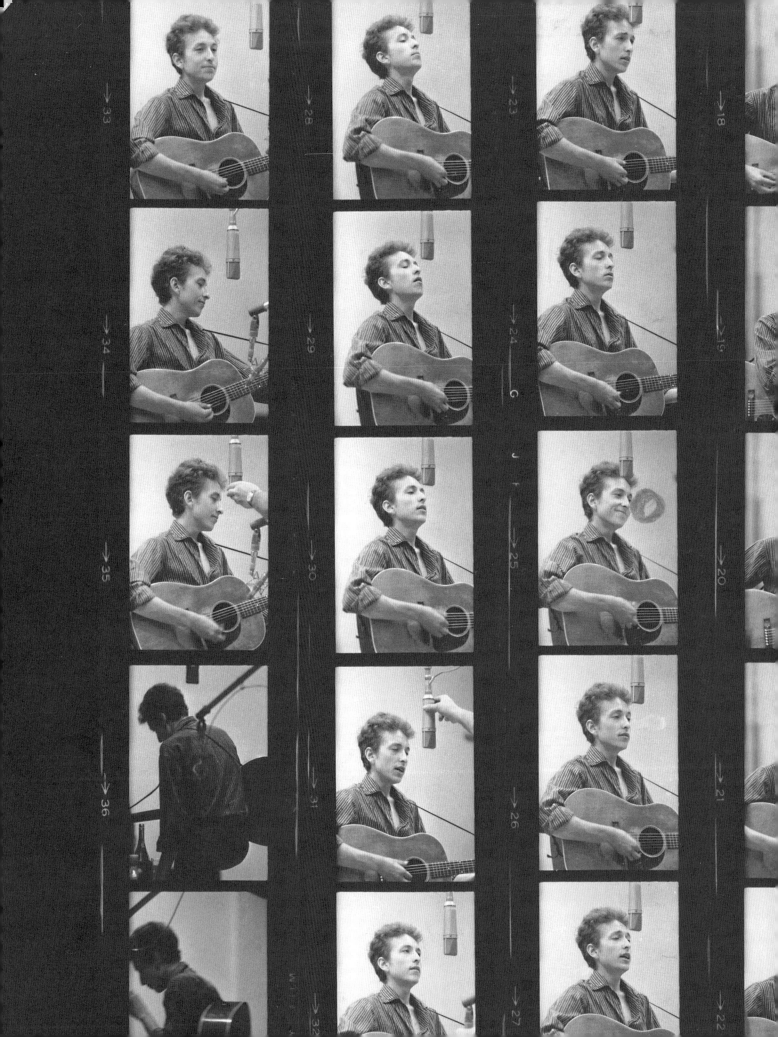